Coping with Un-cope-able Parents

Coping with Un-cope-able Parents

Parents

LOVING ACTION for Eldercare

Carol-Ann Hamilton

BALBOA.
PRESS
A DIVISION OF HAY HOUSE

ISBN: 978-1-4525-5487-7 (sc)
ISBN: 978-1-4525-5488-4 (hc)
ISBN: 978-1-4525-5486-0 (e)

Library of Congress Control Number: 2012912086

Balboa Press books may be ordered through booksellers or by contacting:

Balboa Press
A Division of Hay House
1663 Liberty Drive
Bloomington, IN 47403
www.balboapress.com
1-(877) 407-4847

Because of the dynamic nature of the Internet, any web addresses or links contained in this book may have changed since publication and may no longer be valid. The views expressed in this work are solely those of the author and do not necessarily reflect the views of the publisher, and the publisher hereby disclaims any responsibility for them.

The author of this book does not dispense medical advice or prescribe the use of any technique as a form of treatment for physical, emotional, or medical problems without the advice of a physician, either directly or indirectly. The intent of the author is only to offer information of a general nature to help you in your quest for emotional and spiritual well-being. In the event you use any of the information in this book for yourself, which is your constitutional right, the author and the publisher assume no responsibility for your actions.

Any people depicted in stock imagery provided by Thinkstock are models, and such images are being used for illustrative purposes only.
Certain stock imagery © Thinkstock.

Printed in the United States of America

Balboa Press rev. date: 9/11/2012

Dedicated to:

Kindred Spirits Everywhere
Battling Un–cope–able Parents.

Contents

Foreword

I am the daughter of Un-cope-able Parents. I get that now.

For years I wasn't sure whether it was me. As I matured I recognized it wasn't my fault.

My parents were crazy. They were driving me slowly insane. I'd passed babysitting courses, not eldercare courses. I became a parent. I became a grandparent. I just wasn't prepared to be the caretaker of a nice old lady. We'd officially changed places on the scales of dependence and responsibility. The older we got, the harder it became to know how to maintain a healthy relationship. I was not called upon to handle any diagnosed mental health issues or addictions. My parents were "normal". They called me names in public; forgot my name; cried on my shoulder all night long. They leaned on me emotionally, even before I entered my teens. My dad went bankrupt just months before he died a decade ago. I was the only one of his five children at his side.

Mum can't learn how to use voicemail, digital cameras, computers, e-mail or social media, cell phones or even pierced earrings. She uses VCR's instead of DVD players, horsehair brushes instead of vacuum cleaners. She washes the kitchen floor on her hands and knees and hangs her underwear in the shower to dry. She's absent-mindedly gotten out of a moving vehicle mid-intersection (scaring my daughter-in-law half to death); developed speech impediments, and wants formal invitations to visit us.

My mother shares her apartment with 50 or so plush monkeys and hoards clothes, photos, knick knacks, puzzles. She has talked in circles, stubbornly and loudly clinging to narrow minded opinions on topics about which she knows nothing, then totally contradicting herself. She gossips about every aspect of our lives. Nothing is sacred. She meddles. She frets. The TV is always on, but she rarely reads. Mum refuses to follow her doctor's instructions as she can't understand them, but quotes Dr. Phil or Dr. Oz as gospel when telling us how to live. I thought this was all "normal".

I did freak when my mother opened a new credit card account in my name without telling me. When she authorized a $700 charge on her own credit card over the phone for a cruise vacation she had no intention of taking, it was a nightmare to get reversed. It was my nightmare. My mother has cost me hundreds of dollars in false alarms with the home security system while house sitting and destroyed 'dry clean only' clothes while doing laundry. She doesn't use the apartment freezer or walker we bought her; remembers her childhood but forgets yesterday; alienated the few friends she had and is jealous of mine. She'd planned to move in (again, we tried that once already) without telling me. She's not malicious. Nothing's wrong with this picture, it is situation normal. SNAFU, that is.

As a member of the Baby Boomer generation, I found it very difficult to know how to cope with my parents on top of my full time job, volunteer work, my spouse, my sons, my grandchildren, two houses, two cars and multiple health issues. How does a child cope with parents who don't know how or are unable to show love? Even as an adult I'm still learning; it can feel lonely.

Enter Carol-Ann Hamilton. Carol-Ann is the real deal. I've been fortunate to have her in my life for the past two decades – first as an esteemed colleague in corporate Canada and now as abiding friends. In that time, she has taught me a whole new, humorous way of looking at things. I feel privileged to gain behind-the-scenes looks at the world of this seasoned facilitator and coach. She is a sister of courage who has helped me transition from one stage of my life to another with grace. These days, you'll recognize us as the two middle-aged ladies you see in a downtown restaurant laughing so hard we're crying; it's happened more than once!

As a resident expert, Carol-Ann has been consciously practicing coping strategies with her parents all her adult life and making notes of successful tactics to share with us. She is, as of this writing, still dealing with multiple issues with her father (89 years and counting).

In fact, Carol-Ann coined the phrase "un-cope-able" as the degree of "impossible" she has personally experienced and/or acknowledged in the anecdotes of friends, colleagues and clients like me. She has a unique understanding of the issue and how pervasive (plus invasive!) it is in Canada and around the world today. This dynamic self-help book is the result.

In my opinion, opening a public dialogue on strategies to cope with impossible parents couldn't have happened at a better time. I believe we need to live our "today's" such that our "tomorrows" take care of themselves. We cannot ignore the problems as they'll not go away; they'll just get worse if we do. It's not acceptable for us to make Granny live in the garage, so if we have aged parents or other senior dependents, we must learn how to prevail. Carol-Ann has provided a marvelous tool to guide us.

She knows retirement homes are overcrowded, expensive and often over-rated. She's researched long term care facilities and subsidized nursing residences. She finds home care is preferred for multiple reasons, yet also realizes how much of a strain it puts on family life and relationships. We're all aware of the rise in reports of elder abuse. It's no way to live. It's no way to die. While some of us are thinking about the global social concerns of a growing senior population, and wondering what to do about it, Carol-Ann gives us practical tools to help us retain our sanity today in our personal lives.

She has drawn the many parallels between elderly parents and newborns. Individually we can't exile, abandon or neglect our aged any more than we could an infant. However, this book is not about daycare centers for seniors, or the development of eldercare education, or promoting a foster program for the adoption of lonely old Grannies. It isn't advocating a paid year to care for a senior parent in their final year, like a maternity or paternity leave upon their birth of a child (despite the similar needs). While recognizing the financial and time constraints of making any significant social changes, her focus is on making the most of what we already have control over in the best interests of those who brought us into this world.

Carol-Ann helps us understand our situation, our current relationships and the toll they take on our health and spirit. She provides "loving action" steps to make the best possible peace with your parents. Perhaps they can't or won't change, but you can and will, probably significantly faster than the advocates for social change can catch up with us.

Let's get real now. This book is about you, the reader. Complete the interactive Impossible Parents Questionnaire in this book, as I did. One can hardly read it without answering the questions in one's head and either smiling or laughing out loud in cynical identification with the pathetic patterns most of us experience to some degree. Carol-Ann anticipates and provides intuitive responses to the questions or feelings so very few of us actually voice.

With her insights, we can resolve a great deal with our parents long after we've become adults. We can reconcile our past. We can further address a great deal of conflict within ourselves during our parents' "old age". We can prepare for their future, and for our own.

Carol-Ann identifies the hidden opportunities that exist for all of us in these relationships. We might learn to feel and express gratitude that was previously left unsaid. We may locate that elusive forgiveness so vital to our own well-being. This book may even form the foundation for a new reality show. Carol-Ann arms us, as the warrior woman she is, with tools and resources to ensure that the memories we make between today and the day our parents pass on are good ones.

Through my long association with Carol-Ann, I've watched her develop and implement techniques to literally stop her Un-cope-able Parents from sapping her energy, her very life force. I'm proof her methods work. I'm neither as anxious nor stressed as previously about trying to be the perfect daughter to an imperfect mother. I laugh a lot more, instead of crying out with frustration. I can patiently await my mum's timely end, without feeling guilty for hoping it arrives before we are forced to face the shortfalls of current society (living conditions and available support services).

I can and will let go gracefully in the end, which is in the highest interests of all.

You, too, will relate to the experiences and feelings herein. Relax and enjoy, knowing all's well. I am okay. You are okay. Laughter is the world's best medicine. We are not alone. The soul-enriching stories you'll read in this volume inspire and motivate us to do better, to think. You'll feel reassured in having a roadmap for the journey. You may happily realize you're already well along the path to success. You may detach from your situation and put it into proper perspective. You may discover it isn't as bad as you thought or at least no worse than many others.

I look at my relationship today with my adult son, married with three children, and I think about my tomorrows, also. I dearly wish I could somehow ensure that my children won't suffer legacy relationships with me as I age. Simply put, I don't want to do that to them. I don't want to be "un-cope-able" now or then. I don't want them to be in my position. Things need to change NOW if my sons' experiences with me as an elderly parent are going to be any different from mine. It's not that far away, after all.

If not for this book, the Sandwich Generation could risk becoming the soggy middles in an old burnt (out) triple-decker grilled cheese – and that's no bologna! As next-generation adult caregivers, we're adding one more responsibility to already overwhelming loads. Not a good scenario for fostering positive, productive relationships with our parents, especially if our rapport was at all strained beforehand.

Carol-Ann IS changing the world for the better every day. She is making a difference. She does so through her books, through her teaching, through her coaching, through her writing and general conversations, through just BEING.

I believe the message and techniques she shares in this book are WAY too important to ever lose sight of and have repeatedly told her so. Take the time to internalize this simple, entertaining story to the broader social concerns of an aging population and our relationships with elders.

Follow her continuing saga. Listen to her plea about the future. It's your future, too. Contained in these pages is an opportunity to profoundly change your life.

Michelle Moody,
Advocate for Women Survivors of Violence
Oshawa, Ontario, CANADA

Preface

"I see another book for you."

An apparently-simple statement uttered while sitting in a middle school Staff Room surrounded by beautiful painted wall murals – a legacy left by a beloved principal who had passed away the summer before. Her untimely loss made us all think – deeply.

I admit to being stunned. Here I imagined I was on a consulting assignment. Not really. Not ultimately.

No, in the end, I was meant to bear witness to teachers' heartfelt outpourings about difficult aging parents. I needed to hear their conflicted sharing, as each tale reflected precisely what I'd been enduring since re-entering the family-of-origin fray caused by my mother's exponentially-declining state. Their wrenching stories offered personal healing – along with so much more.

In hindsight, these brief dialogues catalyzed a whole new vista of work.

What I had no idea of then – but have now connected to profoundly – is that a **huge** part of my Earthly mission is to **advocate** on behalf of those in the Sandwich Generation who face agonizing decisions related to our elderly folks. To those perceptive women, I owe my first debt of gratitude.

For, I now see that EVERYTHING in my life surviving Un-cope-able Parents has prepared me to pen this volume. I therefore thank my mother and father – sincerely – for being trying to the mathematical power of Infinity. Without their unapologetic defiance, I would have never arrived at the insights which will help countless millions the world over.

Not for our small family unit the pat answers or simplistic advice rendered by well-intended self-acclaimed sages. Are you kidding?? We are SOOO far beyond the pale of these truisms, it's not even funny.

If you've ever verbally fought just short of coming to actual blows in attempting to *gently* propose it might be time to entertain a next stage of life, I've been there.

If you've ever been met with unquantifiable resistance at the mere *hint* of leaving the residence in which your parent(s) have been located for decades, I've been there.

If you've ever vociferously battled at risk of being disinherited (or at minimum thrown onto the sidewalk) for even *suggesting* to bring into the household caregivers who could offer bare-necessity food and cleaning services, I've been there.

If you've ever done *all* in your level power to support your parents in their wishes and still your full-out capacity comes nowhere close to filling the bottomless pit of their neediness, I've been there.

If you've ever attempted up to the *maximum* limit of your physicality to make their final days peaceful and orderly – yet your *extreme* efforts remain for naught – I've been there.

And that's just the tip of the iceberg! I could go on. But I won't. It would be pointless. All I can say is there's virtually nothing I haven't encountered at the hands of one or both parents.

Despite their over-usage, my mantras are: Been there… Done it… Got the T-shirt!

No, I haven't any academic credentials in the geriatrics field. However, I have vast practical experience. And I have soul. In my view, those are the only ingredients needed to make a positive difference in your situation.

Sure, our stories may take different forms. Yet, if you have Un-cope-able Parents, yours will be largely nerve-wracking encounters. Close to your wit's end, you want to pull out your hair, strand by strand. Am I right? Of course!

You have my earnest empathy. You have my unbridled support. It's for YOU I write.

As with my book, *Step Out of Your Sandbox!* I yearn for you to benefit from my painfully-earned lessons. No victory with my folks has been easy. All have been exceptionally hard-won. If even one idea I've offered based upon my obstinate elders saves you unnecessary anguish, I'll be fulfilled.

Never mind the illuminating accounts friends and colleagues have generously gifted upon invitation for the first time in my writing career. I thank them on bended knee and more acutely than mere words could ever express. You will soon see for yourself what I already know to be true.

For, I can squarely tell you that transcribing their moving narratives has been nothing short of therapeutic. Wow! So often I've lost track, tears streamed down my face while recognizing the torture others suffer at the hands of their challenging elders.

Apart from an infant's relentless demands, I can think of no period on Earth that will leech such tremendous energy from your precious stores. Whether in their actual presence or merely directing psychic attention their way, your Un-cope-able Parents will siphon off your every vestige of physical, emotional and mental stamina.

That is, if you let them. Ah, there's the rub.

Yes, if you'll apply just a few of the many ideas embedded within the LOVING ACTION Keys, I'm certain you'll gain more than a fraction of internal serenity and equanimity. This is so, even if you're dealing with severely Un-cope-able Parents.

As an added bonus – just when you're at the height of despair – I believe you'll find yourself downright astounded. At the very moment of wanting to throw in the towel, the Universe will drop small miracles into your lap. Please relish these rare pleasant twists and turns! I'm sure these out-of-the-blue happenings are sent to sustain us. They've occurred in my father's case. They will come your way, also. Trust me.

In order to receive these treasures, you'll be called forth to summon courageous willingness to initiate powerful conversations of the sort this author and respected contributors have stepped boldly into. I fully realize it can be uncomfortable, painful or downright scary to tread near the subject of death. You're not well-received in those moments. Far from it! As my own stories only too well attest!

Yet, you must – for your sake and that of your Un-cope-able Parents. If only to save them from themselves…

At the time of writing, my father's rate of collapse expands bi-weekly; it used to be measured semi-annually or quarterly. His transition draws nigh.

A cherished friend likened this stage to the final lap of a marathon. How perfect! The runner (you!!!) oozes sweat by the buckets. Panting and almost breathless, the finish line is in sight. It might as well be a million miles away. The exertion has virtually drained your life's blood.

Yet, it's in these last few make-or-break moments that champions are made.

Seconds typically separate the winner from the pack. What were the differentiating factors? Determination. Preparation. Fortitude. Perseverance.

Complicated and multi-faceted for giver and recipient alike, care of the un-manageable aged is surely a race to ultimate "victory". It's not for the faint-hearted.

For those coping with Un-cope-able Parents, the win derives from prevailing – no matter what!! It's resting in the knowingness of having done everything in your level power to rise to your Best Self as your impossible relatives reach the end of life.

My earnest wish is that this volume will leave a profound positive footprint in your individual and familial lives.

Broadly-speaking, I'm delighted to report that my media stacks on the burden eldercare exacts in Canada (and other nations) now grows by the week. We stand at the threshold of an explosive crisis. At the same time, there's an opportunity for global transformation.

Which option will you sign up for?

Carol-Ann Hamilton
Sandwich Generation Advocate & Activist
Toronto, Ontario, CANADA
June 2012

The Impossible Parents Questionnaire

You Have Un-cope-able Parents If...

1. Your eyeballs roll into the farthest reaches of your head at the mere thought of them.
2. You have to spend hours "psyching" yourself up while getting ready to be in their presence.
3. You want to tear out your hair strand by strand before, during and/or after dealing with them (even if have a full head of hair, you'd never possess enough for all you'd like to yank).
4. You grind your teeth to their roots while clamping down on what you'd really wish with all your might to say – and that's just in one phone call!
5. You risk at any moment to lose *all* your accumulated knowledge, wisdom, experience and skill because they manage (for the millionth time) to destroy your capability due to their attitudes, beliefs or actions.
6. You have to endure hours-long diatribes having nothing to do with the subject matter at hand in order to wait to make your key points with one or both folks.
7. You are completely spent – physically, emotionally, mentally and spiritually – on the heels of interacting with them (it doesn't matter whether this is hours or minutes).
8. You have to demonstrate Super-Human powers of perseverance and patience in order to prevail.

9. You know in the deepest places of your interior what is called for to support or make a difference in their elderly lives and they will have none of it.

10. You feel you've attempted every available device known to humankind and yet you make zero headway in influencing them to see your point of view.

Based on what I've shared so far, would it surprise you that it took mere moments to compose these points? Truly!

All I had to do was summon the memories of a parental visit at the time. Boom! Ten easy questions!

As we next move into the audiences for whom this work is intended (as well as those to whom it doesn't apply), I urge you to think about your responses to each of the statements above.

To learn more about how I've successfully addressed each of these stressors, check out the chapter on Question & Answer Time.

Who's This Book For?

You WILL Be Served By This Work If:

- You laugh out loud – no, make that ROAR – in recognition of your circumstances within the Impossible Parents Questionnaire ☺

- You're wondering: *"Am I a secret brother or sister to this woman, because otherwise how could she possibly know our family so well"?*

> *"The light isn't shining enough on me."* (This ironic complaint was uttered by the impossible mother of a friend who makes it her life's work to be the center of attention. On this occasion, an inadequate number of lamps were turned on in her basement lair.)

- You're thinking, *"Finally! Someone on the Planet who 'gets' what it's really like to deal with my folks. Hallelujah!!!"*

- You easily recognize that you're **compelled** to read further because this book contains information you need to receive.

- You draw HOPE from the possibility that there *is* a way to navigate your parental relationship so the highest and best for all concerned can be attained.

You don't necessarily find connection to this extract from *MORE* magazine, dated February/March 2011. Author Karen Hamilton argues that even though looking after an aging parent can be heart-breaking, love conquers all. OK…

Ms. Hamilton remembers standing over a bathroom sink holding her Dad's dentures and seeing her smile reflected back in the bathroom mirror; he'd just thrown up because he had cancer and was dying. She acknowledges she could have felt resentful or disgusted, but in that moment found herself *"privileged"*.

She equally draws out the example of a 52-year-old single mom who waded right into the muck of assisting with her father's bathing to cleaning his colostomy bag – concluding that children who care for elderly parents find it *"fulfilling and affirming"*.

Further, the author goes on to subtly deride images conjured up by the word, caregiver. To quote, *"I envision a worn-out woman caring for her elderly, cranky parents; she's doing her best but barely getting by, isolated, angry and tired. One notch up from crazy cat lady, she's somebody nobody wants to be."*

Helloooo!!!! Have I just entered some kind of weird alternative reality? Last time I looked, I haven't (yet) turned into some kooky eccentric that people cross to the other side of the street to avoid simply because I practically gag in the face of such self-righteousness. That is, unless someone isn't telling me something!

Count me amongst those 70 per cent of (mostly) women who consider tending to head-strong parents stressful and who are worried the pressure might do us in. In its defense, the article goes on to report that caregivers who experience such tension have a higher mortality rate – 63 per cent – than non-caregivers of the same age. Thank you for the concession.

YOU WILL NOT RELATE IF:

- You've never experienced any of the above behaviors or attitudes.

- You're right now saying to yourself: *"I love my parents. They're perfect — whether passed away or alive. What are you talking about, Carol-Ann?"*

- You have difficulty acknowledging you're in the minority of the population if you have no such issues with your folks. Lucky you! Be glad. Please never take your situation for granted in a self-congratulatory way.

- Your folks fit images like the photograph of a granny singing group featured in a local magazine called The Hurricanes; these ladies look like they've totally got it "going on" even in their matronly attire — electric guitars in hand and one pounding her drums with gusto in the background!

- Your parents' attitudes parallel that of a 91-year-old senior who makes his own bread at home — and does 24 sit-ups plus push-ups a day. I don't even do that, for Heaven's sake! This gentleman can't see but he's just moved houses, and doesn't *"plan on sitting around all day"*.

- Or, your Mom is like this alpha-grandmother depicted by Howie Kahn in a December 2010 O magazine article. Initially shut down when her husband passed away in 1965, she now holds court at the seniors' home. Votes are cast to determine who is permitted to sit at her dining room table. Should a resident doze off in the lobby, Grandma indignantly vocalizes: *"It makes it look like old people live here. If they want to sleep, they should go back to their beds."* (Now, I do recognize that Un-cope-able Parents come in all guises,

3

and you may find this lady's harsh strictures over-the-top. What irks in one family may not annoy in another.) I personally admire her feisty nature, having wished my own mother had possessed more backbone.

- You secretly or overtly condemn statements within the Impossible Parents Questionnaire in this fashion: *"Wow. What is her problem? She's talking about the two people who gave her life. She has no right to her feelings."*

- You entertain no other possibility (should your parents ever become incapacitated) than to house them in your own environment because that is what children "should" do in order to look after those who brought them into this world.

On the other hand, those for whom this work is **geared** will immediately recognize this final bullet is something you will **never** entertain – to bring one or (God forbid!!) both into your sacred space. Over your dead body! For, you know you'd be giving up your last remnants of balance and sanity – maybe even tethering to this world!

Of Note: Even those couples in my circles who willingly assumed the admirable stance of taking in their loved ones wound up temporarily dissolving their marital bliss until after Dad and Mom passed away.

The "Case" for This
Information – Now!

Tell me something I don't know! Like I would need to spell out a rationale as to why this book is needed IMMEDIATELY...

Just examine these facts and figures:

- In 2009, there were 4.7 million seniors in Canada (or about 13.9% of the population). Between 2031 and 2036, that number is expected to climb to 10.9 million (or about 25% of the projected population). These figures can be found in a House of Commons newsletter report (summer 2010).

  > *"The crisis is not 10 years down the road. We're talking even today..."* (Health Council of Canada CEO, John Abbott, in the *Toronto Sun*, April 16, 2012 as written by Jessica Murphy of the Parliamentary Bureau)

- In 1971, there were nearly 8 persons of working age for every Canadian over 65. By 2008, that ratio had fallen to 5.1. By 2019, it will be 3.8 and by 2033, that number will have shrunken to 2.5. These forecasts are troubling for many reasons – not the least of which concern an alarming dearth of young people to support a burgeoning mature populace. Old age security, pension plans and healthcare will be taxed to the hilt – likely to a breaking point if radical alterations aren't undertaken in the present.

- While the purpose of this volume is not to digress into a diatribe about government actions required to mitigate faltering systems, I cannot pass by this story. It confirms the dire need for this book. Unimaginable! In October 2011, *National Post* newspaper commentator Christie Blatchford prominently featured the despicable hospital experiences of an 82-year-old lady. Leaving her dying husband's bedside, she fell in the lobby and was left lying face-down with a broken hip and badly-bleeding arm. People stepped over and around her for 28 minutes. "Protocol" required that 911 be called and an ambulance dispatched before she could be attended to. Unbelievable!

• Pivotally, the *Toronto Star* issued a front-page article in February 2012 entitled, *"Ontario says tougher rules expected for drivers with dementia"*. This was released at the very moment my increasingly-incapacitated widowed 89-year-old father was preparing to renew his auto insurance – on both vehicles! Tough new rules, better training for family doctors on reporting cognitively impaired patients and more rigorous on-road testing of senior drivers both inflamed and doused the fire on my father's ill-conceived plans. I could have kissed the ground these staff reporters walk on for highlighting this **critical** issue. It was like a magic wand had been waved from Above, giving me merciful ammunition to make a successful argument where none had previously existed.

• Infuriated to learn that Ontario is one of the last jurisdictions in North America to embrace "de-graduated" licenses for seniors I immediately hopped onto the newspaper's website plus my Facebook page to issue my own edicts! Namely, whether we're talking days (for teenagers) or decades (for seniors), incompetence behind the wheel of any sort is literally a matter of life and death!! Period.

- To further reinforce the "OMG, is he or she still driving" stage of life, an editorial in the *Canadian Medical Association Journal* dated April 2, 2012 called anew for licensing adjustments. Author Donald Redelmeier, a professor of medicine at the University of Toronto, suggests a full driver's license automatically default to restricted access once seniors reach a certain age (to be determined). At that point, he proposes capable drivers can resume full driving privileges if a physician certifies their good health.

- Even though the editorial cites a Transport Canada report that says 389 of the 2,209 Canadians who died in vehicle accidents in 2009 were over 65 (higher than any other age group), a respondent labeled graduated licensing *"age discrimination"*. So be it! Somebody needs to have the guts to do something here – medically or otherwise. Redelmeier's thesis is to reframe interactions between seniors and their doctors by positioning the physician to endorse a full driver's license rather than revoke privileges. My parents' doctor failed to put down her foot; perhaps this direction would help her in being less spineless.

- Despite almost-daily frustrations with my Un-cope-able Parent, the tragic issue of elder abuse is featured regularly on TV and in written form. For example, an ad sponsored by www.seniors.gc.ca depicts disturbing scenes of emotional cruelty; I'm always saddened upon viewing it.

- A government report echoes this hidden crime often goes undetected; up to 10% of seniors experience it. Whether physical, emotional, financial or abandonment by families or institutions, elder abuse is a disturbing societal problem. I'm convinced these statistics will climb if children of seniors don't get effective help for coping with challenging parents – as found in my writing along with other resources.

- From time to time, one comes across an eloquent article that offers awareness while tugging on heart-strings, such as this banner: *"Crisis often leads to clean-up"*. Accompanied by photos of a cluttered living room that can only be termed atrocious with piles and filth, it shows an "extreme cleaner" wearing protective gear whose job is to remove health and other hazards so dangerous to seniors with mobility and cognitive impairments. Incredible! I believe this will be a dramatically-growing profession. The expert indicates: *"Many are simply overwhelmed by life, depressed at growing frail and fiercely clinging to reminders of friends and family who have died before them"*. Holding on to stuff is almost a way of holding onto the past.

- Then, there are miscellaneous informative pieces: dealing with aging parents can ignite old rivalries, imploring siblings to cooperate to ensure ailing parents get effective care; how taking in an elderly parent will have emotional, physical and financial ramifications for a family; how dementia can (poignantly) bring ex-partners together; tax-time recommendations to claim significant expenditures in order to ease the monetary burdens associated with caring for a loved one with dementia; the advantages of doling out inheritances while still alive.

- Since beginning this book, a franchise called Nurse Next Door has started up to provide companionship, medical and personal care plus registered nursing to those in need. I strongly feel such home healthcare services will be a salvation-boon to many.

- In fact, Canada and the U.S. are far from the only nations facing daunting elder issues. Although WWII resulted in an unspeakably tragic loss of life, take in this newspaper article about Japan's corpse hotels. I kid you not! Graphically, it points out the average wait time for an oven is over four days in Yokohama, driving up demand for these half-way morgues. For a flat fee, bereaved families can check in their dead while in-queue for one of the city's overworked crematoriums. Death is apparently a rare booming market in stagnant Japan. Like a "wild west", as the content compares.

• In 2040, annual deaths in Japan are expected to peak at 1.66 million as the bulk of the nation's Baby Boomer generation expires. I suspect figures are similar around the globe, wherever post-war population explosions resulted in a bulging Sandwich Generation.

• From time to time, inspiring pieces also reach me. Check out this *Toronto Star* newspaper report on a groundbreaking study which will follow 50,000 people between the ages of 45 and 85 over a 20-year period. Experts will collect information on the changing biological, medical, psychological, social and economic aspects of their lives. The aim is to unlock some of the greatest mysteries of aging – and the many influencing factors – so researchers can find ways to improve Canadians' health. As the study's lead principal investigator professor Parminder Raina of McMaster University in Hamilton states: *"We're looking at the aging process from cell to society."*

No matter what...

YOU – between The Greatest Generation (as Tom Brokaw refers to it in his 2001 classic *An Album of Memories*) and your own growing families – are the ones toward whom this work is targeted. You daily experience the **unremitting** demands of managing the care of young and old alike.

Sure, there's ample professional content out there about how to achieve productive outcomes with an aging population. Plenty of resources...

lots of great information… advice galore. Updates on federal legislation and regulations affecting seniors, funding opportunities, legal reports and more…

Then, there's "reality".

Where are the helpful tips written from the perspective of your **feelings** about eldercare? Not so much.

Here, we're talking about expertise that addresses in a **practical** manner how you cope with issues referenced in the Impossible Parents Questionnaire.

Now, I must admit… I claim no formal qualifications to write about this subject matter. I haven't University degrees in this realm, which we all know is the ubiquitously-accepted credential. My businesses are not centered upon psycho-therapy, medicine or leading-edge hospice practices.

Still, those for whom this content is **truly** intended will easily and readily agree you can research all the clinically-proven tomes in the world. Yet, this will do **nothing** to change what you know in your deepest core to be true…

…There is **zilch** any documented professional can say or write that you haven't already long ago thought of to contend with your particular family dynamics. They can render all the well-meant wisdom in the world. Unfortunately, this will do nothing to alter your picture.

Why?? Because you've already tried everything!!

You will instantly identify the following suggestions as genuine efforts from friends and colleagues who don't know better. These unsophisticated offerings come in the form of questions like: *"Why don't you___"*, *"Have you ever considered___"* and *"How about___"* Fill in the blanks with conventional advice like putting them into an assisted living facility and calling additional support or resources into their home on a consistent basis.

Please! Give you more credit than that!!

If we were merely talking about time-worn truisms regarding what to do for your intractable aging parents (and how to do it), you'd have solved all your issues eons ago!

Am I right? Certainly!

Two Keys to Coping

WHAT DOESN'T WORK

Even if no one else validates your feeling of *"Duh...Been there, done it"*, I'm here without a doubt to acknowledge you've already tested the following in a (vain) attempt to influence and persuade your stubborn folks to entertain wise alternatives that support their increasing health and other needs:

- Abdicate (your needs)
- Beg
- Cajole
- Demand
- Explain (logically)
- Force
- Grovel
- Humiliate
- Insult
- Jump (up and down in frustration)
- "Kill" (as in, wanting to kill them some days)
- Lie
- Manipulate
- Name-call
- Over-ride
- Plead
- Quarrel
- Retaliate
- Shout
- Train (as in, educate)
- Undermine
- Vanquish

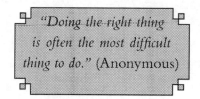

"Doing the right thing is often the most difficult thing to do." (Anonymous)

- Wrong
- X-acerbate
- Yell
- Zeal (demonstrate)

It's like an A to Z compendium of what doesn't work! And, you could probably come up with multiples of your own A to Z lists.

If the matter were as straight-forward as that, I reinforce – you'd have long ago succeeded. Isn't that so??

WHAT DOES WORK

Alright then, what AM I suggesting you do? If you've already tried everything and it hasn't worked, what's left? I hear you!

Would you like the answer? Apply LOVING ACTION.

"You can't possibly be serious', you're thinking. After all the research... After all the evidence... After all the documentation...*"That's about as much as you have for me, Carol-Ann?"*

I'm afraid so.

On the other hand, isn't it rather a relief you "only" have to keep in mind these two acronyms? How "easy" is that?? At least the tenets will be quickly recalled when it's time to use them. Now, hear me right. I'm not saying they're a cinch to implement. Why? Because you have Un-cope-able Parents!

Oh to have acquiescent, sensible and logical parents — "normal" folks. No, no, no. Not for you. Alas, you drew the short end of the proverbial straw and got resistant, immature elders.

Believe you me. I know of what I speak here!

My own mother and father respectively resided and stand at the **extreme** end of the unreasonable spectrum. Just ask my small family of relatives and a few trusted intimates if you're assuming right now, *"it can't be that bad."* Oh **yes** it can!

No stone remains unturned in terms of the strategies I've tried with them. Akin to an out-of-control pendulum that swings wildly from side to side, I've attempted the level-headed and ridiculous, the rational and irrational — and everything between.

Within the assertiveness training I do in corporate Canada, we talk about how, when learning to release unassertiveness, people frequently go from mealy-mouthed to aggressive — by-passing the preferred attitudes and actions of assertiveness altogether. This is a predictable pattern.

Through **extensive** personal experience, I've discovered a parallel with non-compliant aging parents. Namely, it's quite possible to go from passive hands-off mindsets to aggressive overly-controlling methods — missing a whole range of more suitable choices along the way.

What makes me so sure? I've experimented with them all!

And I've also failed – always miserably – at any ploys remotely smacking of my negativity or hidden agendas. Not that I didn't try to force-fit or inflict my program upon the pair right up until all unconstructive endeavors proved fruitless.

After the massive trial and error, I can attest the only techniques that generated lasting impact are LOVING ACTION.

LOVING

LOVING Stands For

L – Laughter

O – Openness

V – Vibration

I – Intention

N – Neutrality

G – Grace

Do you notice anything about the elements of LOVING?

Correct! They're attitudes, qualities and characteristics. Each represents a state of **Being**. This is by design.

That's because the frenetic North American culture places such an over-emphasis upon Doing that we forget all effective action ought to be consistently preceded by **deliberate intent**.

The prescribed sequence flows as follows:

- **Be** (first consciously embody positive feelings and beliefs toward your parents)
- **Do** (then perform the requisite actions)
- **Have** (the end result being the quality of care and relationship you seek for and with your loved ones)

Not the other way around, regardless of how typical it is to wire up this process backwards in fast-paced societies.

You see, our crazy-busy lives have us mostly default to action over reflection. It's almost like any action is valued over no action at all. While this bias does avoid "analysis paralysis", can we agree ill-considered deeds easily make your situation worse!

That's why we're going to focus on each of the six Being states in detail – first – as we get underway.

In so doing, I'll be drawing from my own 100% true illustrations, unfathomable as some of them may sound. It's the same with friends' examples.

Even though an only child (which magnifies the burden of responsibility upon one set of shoulders), I know my advice for those readers who do have siblings is spot-on. Too many of you with brothers and sisters have relayed an archetype whereby the care-giving weight seems to inevitably fall upon one sibling – for reasons of geography, convenience, abdication or others.

For more understanding, see the chapters called You're Not Alone Anymore and My Story.

Laughter

Let's start by returning to the Impossible Parents Questionnaire.

Did you happen to notice a number of items referenced how *crazy* your parents can make you? As in, their nuttiness so drives you over the edge some days, you risk becoming as loony as they can be!

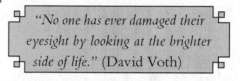

"No one has ever damaged their eyesight by looking at the brighter side of life." (David Voth)

Thus, if you can't locate humor in the situation, you're in peril of going insane! After all, some or a lot of what you deal with is so completely ludicrous that if you tried to intelligently explain it to those who don't get it, they'd think you were the zany one.

Take, for example, a crisis with one of my friends' mothers who suffered from Alzheimer's disease. Let me state upfront that a parental emergency is **by no means** a laughing matter. Rather, it's the kernel of humor within this story that constitutes my point.

Having just fallen in her room, the care facility immediately called an ambulance to take her to Emergency. The threat of hip fracture was very real. Naturally, everyone involved was extremely concerned until the ordeal was over and she was released from hospital with no breakage. How lucky!

Understandably, it took some days for my girlfriend to calm down after this latest trial within a progressively-declining maternal life span. Only then could she recount the lighter side of an otherwise devastating scenario.

Again, please appreciate I am not making fun of Alzheimer's patients! Anyone who lives with or knows someone suffering from this terrible disease knows first-hand its debilitating impacts. I merely transcribe here.

Apparently, when Janet★ (names changed) visited her Mom in the aftermath of the fall and shared how happy she was that all turned out well, her mother turned to her in disbelief, *"What ambulance? What fall? What are you talking about? Are you crazy?"* Like there had never been all this kerfuffle around her mother just days before. I can happily say Janet was hollering in gales of laughter over such incredulity when we shared our coffees.

She realized what all of us should bear in mind. If you can't manage to locate some lightness, you might as well curl up in the fetal position and work yourself into an endless crying jag. It doesn't matter whether you're a woman or man.

Not that there isn't a time and place for tears. Indeed, there's genuine sadness in bearing witness to the deterioration of a parent who once looked after you.

All we're offering under Laughter as a sanity strategy is to find what's bizarre in the circumstances (on a certain level) so you can remain strong yourself.

What's the choice? You could succumb to the lunacy, I suppose. Which option do you think will serve you – and your parents – better?

To supplement my experience that laughter is the best medicine, I hope you enjoy these light tidbits commensurate with the rise of social media. It's predicted that increasing numbers of senior citizens will text and tweet. For this aging demographic (which the Baby Boomers will eventually join), I offer a series of codes for your amusement:

ATD: At The Doctor's

BTW: Bring the Wheelchair

CUATSC: See You at the Senior Center

DWI: Driving While Incontinent

FWIW: Forgot Where I Was

GGPBL: Gotta Go, Pacemaker Battery Low!

GHA: Got Heartburn Again

IMHO: Is My Hearing-Aid On?

LMDO: Laughing My Dentures Out

ROFL...CGU: Rolling On the Floor Laughing...And Can't Get Up

TTYL: Talk to You Louder

WTP: Where's The Prunes?

Openness

Now, this one is a tricky balancing act.

I'm not suggesting you go into your parental dealings wide open – energetically speaking. In fact, the grounded methods you apply to deal with difficult corporate matters represent the same muscle I'm suggesting to cope with impossible parents. After all, you wouldn't go into a contentious meeting with your boss unprepared.

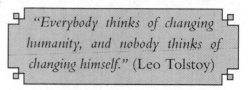

"Everybody thinks of changing humanity, and nobody thinks of changing himself." (Leo Tolstoy)

Quite the contrary! You need a proper amount of surrounding "plating" so as to not be left vulnerable and exposed in the face of difficult elders. Think spiritual warrior preparing to do battle.

Toward that end, I've instituted a new ritual when my husband Derek and I approach my father's neighborhood these days. Though not a Star Trek fan myself, I've adopted from Captain Picard: *"Shields up."* We laugh our heads off!

Kooky as it might sound, I find the expression serves as a helpful declaration and reminder to maintain my boundaries around him. Otherwise, I'm in real danger of coming away even more weakened than is already the case from what can only be described as grueling visits.

For you, too, the threat is to reduce into that still-small tender Child within who lacks the power to cope, if you don't remember to carry such protection. Do you know what I mean? Have your friends or spouse ever given you feedback on this? Mine has. Years ago, my hubby observed – astutely – that I temporarily regressed to Little Carol-Ann on parental visits even though a successful business woman in my own right by then. And that was during so-called normal times. Never mind now – which contain some truly outrageous periods with my Dad.

Despite all these words of wisdom about energetic shields and such, I want you to avoid drawing rigid lines in the sand. Stay open to the possibility that there exist many potential perspectives on your folks.

This advice comes straight from my studies through The Coaches Training Institute (CTI). CTI's term, process coaching, refers to taking our clients through a brainstorm of varied perspectives on any given topic. Its purpose is to demonstrate there's always more than one way to look at a situation. The range can extend from positive to negative to neutral and pretty much anything in the middle. Process coaching has the effect of broadening outlook and putting the client at ultimate choice.

If we then transfer this same technique to your Un-cope-able Parents, I have to assume you wish to select lovingly powerful viewpoints. You want to be the kind of son or daughter who takes the high road so you can always look back and say you exemplified your worthy ideals during your parents' pending transitions. Am I right? Of course!

You get to that result by generating your own comprehensive list of attitudes and behaviors by which you would portray your folks. You may even want to carry out this exercise across more than one sitting. Follow your brainstorming with a considered final choice of term(s) that honor you and them.

I'm not ashamed to confess my first list contained some rather derogatory descriptors. In my shoes, you'd see why. Eventually, maturity won the day. I determined that a more charitable set of monikers was in keeping with my True Self.

But this was not until after I'd given myself the liberty of spilling a degree of venom onto paper. I offer you the same freedom. Last I looked, we're all human! I say, it's a necessary part of the journey.

Vibration

Esther and Jerry Hicks in *The Vortex* continue to hold the prize (in my mind) for the most outstanding work in the field of reclaiming Who We Really Are and operating daily at the highest 'vibration' in the decisions we make plus actions we take.

> *"You don't have to work at being in the high vibration that is natural to you, because it is natural to you. But you do have to stop holding the thoughts that cause you to lower your vibration. It's a matter of no longer giving your attention to things that don't allow your cork to float or don't allow you to vibrate in harmony with who you really are."* (Esther and Jerry Hicks)

By vibration, we mean the invisible beliefs we carry that translate directly into all facets of our lives through the people plus experiences we encounter. If you want to get a sense for your vibration (or energy aura), just observe how everyone and everything shows up around you.

At a low vibration, you will attract – like a magnet or TV station emitting a particular frequency – poor relationships and seemingly-constant problems. The opposite goes for a high vibration; things fall into place with ease and grace.

So, how does this Hicks principle tie into coping with Un-cope-able Parents?

For instance, I've noticed a direct correlation between the vibration I carry toward my father during our calls or visits and the energy he reflects back via our interactions. If I'm somehow cranky or impatient, he becomes more entrenched in his stuck ways. When I demonstrate compassion and tolerance, he becomes collaborative.

Perhaps this doesn't strike you as rocket science. Yet, how often do we, in the heat of the 'fight' with Un-cope-able Parents throw up our hands – creating a losing stand-off where everyone retreats to their respective corners to pout, etc.

Borrowing another CTI term, we talk about every person being in their deepest recesses *"whole, resourceful and creative"*. This phrase denotes that everyone possesses on the inside answers to any question or dilemma in their lives. If we're all spirits having a human experience (and not the other way around) then each of us must encompass similar wisdom. That includes your parents. Hard as that may be to accept some days!

Imagine what would be possible if you considered your folks capable in their Essence – even if they don't necessarily operate in this fashion on the surface. Do you believe they'd act differently if you appealed to their inner core?

Remember – they'll show up as morons or adults depending on how you treat them. Just being blunt!

If I may, it has become especially important to maintain a high vibration while partnering with my father in his waning years. For, we need to actively move the needle regarding increasing levels of required support inside and out of the home. If I lose my shape vibration-wise, then both of us lose. I prefer to remain mindful.

Intention

Building on what we said about Vibration, Intention is another potent tool at your disposal. Intention is about the motivation(s) beneath a given course of action.

> *"The remarkable thing is, we have a choice everyday regarding the attitude we will embrace for that day."* (Charles Swindoll)

In the case of your parents, your top-level intentions undoubtedly include: appropriate care; living arrangements; and an interest in their quality of life. Your bottom-line aim is to ensure that the right thing is done to make their remaining days the best possible. Yes? For sure!

Here's a curious thing about intentions, however. You can always discern someone's true motives by what actually happens. For example, you could say you want only the tops for your folks. Then, if the worst occurs, one might legitimately inquire, what was the real intention?

To expand, let me reveal this aspect of my father's hidden agenda toward my mother. On the surface, he'll claim until death that he wished only to do what was right by Mommy. Given her rapidly-worsening state, it was abundantly clear she should have been hospitalized or placed into a chronic care setting. While fully the fitting thing to do, he would have none of it.

No, he was adamant about keeping her in the family home they'd occupied for close to 50 years. No matter what the cost to her well-being, to be honest. Yes, a caregiver came into their residence at least twice a day along with increasing supplementary ministrations near the end. My reflections remain; his wasn't necessarily the most ethical course of action.

What happened? Rigorous examination reveals that my father wanted to do what was convenient by him. It wasn't about Mommy at all. It simply didn't suit him to visit her outside the home. Thus, his selfishness was allowed to dominate.

Naturally, you could ask about my husband and me in this mix. With equal strictness toward myself, my secret motive was to avoid intervening in the whole mess. Perfect hindsight obviously has me conclude I would have done things differently with a second chance. I live with it, and it is a lesson.

Be therefore very careful to examine your interior with diligence to test the purity of your intentions.

Connecting back to the Hicks before moving on to Neutrality, another of their key distinctions is between The Wanted and The Unwanted. In other words, consider what you do want to happen in the scenario. Its opposite is about what you don't want to transpire.

Jerry and Esther counsel – and I unequivocally agree – that we'd be well-advised to focus upon what we *do* want (i.e., positively intend) to occur – in this case, the care of elderly parents. The rationale being, whether you place your attention on what is or is not wanted, you'll receive exactly that. Unwanted brings more unwanted. Intentionality applied to what is wanted naturally leads to beneficial results.

A testament to our tremendous power to literally create our lives!

Neutrality

Returning to the world of coaching, we talk there about assuming a *"charge-neutral"* stance – particularly in the face of challenging people and situations. By this term, we mean

> *"It isn't the mountains ahead to climb that wear you out, it's the pebble in your shoe."* (Mohammed Ali)

you maintain a level of detachment, as opposed to getting all worked-up with strong opinions and emotions one way or the other. You remain peaceful.

As it regards your Un-cope-able Parents, I can hardly imagine a more **charged** topic on Earth than those two! Good grief! Otherwise, you wouldn't be reading this book.

Can't the mere mention of their names send you into a flood of judgments and memories related to when they've been great, good, bad, ugly and indifferent? All these 'labels' we impose upon them...

In our context, a charge-neutral stance would ideally consist of gaining full internal command of all ten elements within the Impossible Parents Questionnaire (for more, see Question and Answer Time). Specifically, this would entail no more eye-ball rolling or "psyching up" to be with them. The depletion of your energy reserves along with hair-pulling would be a thing of the past. You'd find ways to locate your self in their Essence with ease and grace – truly looking out on the world through their eyes.

Fundamentally, you'd engage in all family dialogues with no opinions about what your parents *should* be (or have been), what they *should* do or how their situation *should* be resolved. That's correct. I said *zero* opinions.

Right here, let me express my gratitude to coach, Martha Beck of O magazine for her July 2011 column, called *"I Don't Care"*. When referencing phrases like "loving without caring" and "detached attachment", Beck makes the critical point that caring – with its shades of sadness, fear and insistence – is not love. Yes, to care for someone can mean to adore them, feed them and tend their wounds. But care can also signify sorrow, as in "bowed down by cares" (e.g. anxiety).

Beck adds that when care appears, unconditional love often vanishes. Her notion is that real healing and real love come from people who are both totally committed to helping and still able to emotionally detach.

How perfect! That's **precisely** what we're talking about!

Sure, your parents' cooperation would be lovely, but you don't absolutely need it to experience a given emotional state. This can be incredibly hard to accept. If only others would do what we want! No more!

How would it be to welcome this new belief system that even if your pig-headed parents temporarily render you insane, you can still find joys to embrace?

Before moving along to Grace, I would be remiss if I didn't admit that loving detachment has been an ongoing struggle in my father's care. It's not an easy balance to strike. For, I increasingly **do** have opinions about what *should* be done for him. That said, I practice in offering my ideas without attachment – putting them "out there" and then letting go when he (inevitably) rejects them.

Those who are parents yourselves may find the best comparison in the wisdom of allowing your children to learn their own lessons. You know 'better' but they will not 'get it' until they learn the hard way.

You can lead a horse to water but you can't…make him drink.

Grace

Without question, you've heard the term, grace under pressure. If there were ever a life chapter when graciousness is called for, this is it! According to the Oxford English

> *"When I accept myself as I am, I change. When I accept others as they are, they change."* (Carl Rogers)

Reference Dictionary, graciousness encompasses being kind, indulgent and merciful. It further alludes to "beneficence toward inferiors".

Let's be clear. I'm by no stretch accusing your elders or mine of being inferior. Nonetheless, as they age, many become rather child-like, do they not? In that state, they need to be parented themselves. It's one of the compounding cruxes you're contending with.

To stick-handle these delicate dialogues, you'd be smart to pack in your duffle bag large doses of the skill called self-management. Self-mastery necessitates overcoming your own issues in order to be fully present to your folks' needs. No matter whether your boss is driving you up the wall at work or your children are acting up at home, you must in that moment set aside what's going on with you to be with them.

Or else you're going to miss opportunities to make a positive difference by lowering parental distress levels that can apparently arise out of the blue and blow through the roof like that.

Let me disclose the story I henceforth refer to as "The Missing Glasses Episode" and you'll see what I mean.

So, there my father and I are in the middle of our almost-daily calls when he declares, *"My eyeglasses have gone missing. Someone must have stolen them or possibly we have mice…"* OK (with a hugely-disbelieving bubble above my head)… Now, I'm thinking on my feet, *"How do I respond to such kookiness and unwind this latest sudden crisis in the household?"*

Listen first, ask questions later!

I knew well enough he'd collected days' before all his eye gear in one location in the recreation room so as to have them organized for an upcoming optometrist appointment. Let's not even discuss why he keeps sports glasses he wasn't likely to use at age 88 anymore – unless he secretly plans to yet become the oldest player in the National Hockey League! I guffaw!

In any case, to entirely appreciate this account, you need to know his mountains of "stuff" in that one room alone are so monstrous it takes the finely-honed suppleness of a cat's navigational abilities to maneuver the rickety circuit at the best of times. Can you picture, hoarders on steroids?? Gosh… It proves easy for me to understand how moving the flimsy pile from the pillar of the bar counter to the post of a neighboring couch likely resulted in them toppling onto the floor underneath.

No sooner had we ended our call on a note of us thinking overnight about what could have happened, than the phone rang anew fifteen minutes later. Sure enough! My father found the stack right where I'd suspected – still rather doubtful they might not have been carried off by a rodent!

Thank the Lord I possessed the grace not to inquire whether he'd also lost a novel at the hands of the "reading" varmint! As well as the discretion to hold my tongue from blurting: *"Of all the items in that home worth stealing do you logically think a burglar would go first to your collection of orphaned 1960's and 1970's sun, reading and driving glasses, Daddy?"*

Grace under pressure to rise up and reframe the desperation you feel dealing with your trying-to-the-hilt parents into compassion…

ACTION

ACTION Stands For

A – Advocate

C – Clarify

T – Trust

I – Initiate

O – Observe

N – [I]Nnovate

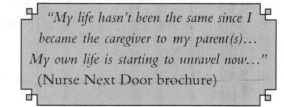

> *"My life hasn't been the same since I became the caregiver to my parent(s)... My own life is starting to unravel now..."* (Nurse Next Door brochure)

So, where are we?

By this point, you've hopefully garnered laser-clarity about your desired level of internal energetic **Vibration** plus **Intentions** before taking even the first active step in your parents' care and handling. You're going to need to be at your prime – and then some.

If you can't bring yourself to a position of **Neutrality** and **Openness**, how far do you think you'll get before you slip into tell-mode and judgment?

And you now know where that leads – straight to attachment and narrow-mindedness. You've been there before. How has that worked for you? Not too well, right? Review the A to Z list for a refresher.

Finally, let's not forget **Laughter** and **Grace**. We all know the physical, emotional and mental benefits of humor. Plus, gracious is how I know you secretly wish to be in the face of this frustrating duo. I 'see' your Essence.

Only after you've consciously reflected on HOW you prefer to BE with your folks, ought you to even think about the ACTION called for. Remember: We're talking about targeted effort here – not the usual ill-considered ready-fire-aim approach of any action for action's sake.

Just as I'm quite certain there's little to no formal documentation devoted to your internal state-of-being regarding Un-cope-able Parents in the manner described here, so too am I sure my recommended actions aren't particularly elaborated within the traditional literature on the subject.

Let's go ahead and break down this second acronym.

Advocate

Right off the bat, I'm not using this term as would care-giving professions. The accepted advice is that family members need

> *"There are two ways of spreading light: to be the candle or the mirror that reflects it."* (Edith Wharton)

to advocate with hospitals or external agencies on behalf of their loved ones to light a fire under authorities' you-know-what's. This is because so many health systems (even Canada's touted government-run model) basically guarantee only the squeakiest wheel gets the grease.

I get that. My point takes a different direction.

Advocate for our purposes means you create a safe environment where *both* parents have the floor to speak their needs with you as their mediator. Cast your mind toward children and teenagers, between whom a squabble can ignite in about two seconds flat!

Just like you had to intervene as the only sane one in the room during that era, so too do you need to be the channel through which each parent's truth flows. For, if your scenario is anything like mine, it's quite possible one of your folks strives to dominate by imposing their will at every juncture.

Let's return to my parents' highly-structured marriage. You can just imagine how hard and long my father argued to keep my mother bed-ridden in their home right until her last breath. During her more lucid moments along the pathway to decrepitude, my husband and I are 100% certain we could have persuaded Mommy (willingly) to go into a long-term care residence.

Recall, though, my ulterior motive was to avoid confrontation and involvement. Thus, I was only too happy to accede to his dictatorial voice. And, my father was delighted to grip the reins of power in his controlling hands. No questions asked.

Do you start to see the under-belly of Intention? Had my genuine spirit been one of stopping at nothing to ensure the best possible outcome for my mother, a very different conversation would have ensued. It's the strategy I offer with respect in 20/20 hindsight to you.

Have you ever encountered times in your career where you've been called upon to bring together two corporate warring factions? I have. And, I'd access the very same process we used to resolve feuding tension between Sales and Customer Service to cope with your Un-cope-able Parents.

Essentially, we facilitated several meetings – one at which only Service was permitted to air their beefs while Sales listened. At the next, roles were reversed. Only at the third meeting were both entities allowed to engage in two-way dialogue. Ultimately, it took about four to five sessions to generate a mutually-satisfactory game plan. Even then, ongoing monitoring was required to prevent slippage into unproductive behavior patterns. The entire series was labor-intensive – yet worth it. Everyone bought in and we achieved win-win results all around.

What was demanded of us as facilitators to obtain these outcomes? For one, we needed to remain neutral and open in order to invite every individual's perspective to the proverbial table. Completely the Being states we've already covered… Had our mediation team been off in Never Land while these critical discussions occurred, it's a surefire bet the conclusions reached wouldn't have addressed everyone's requests.

Given my father's vested agenda in the status quo, Derek and I should have represented – and strongly so – my mother's wishes. It would have taken significant commitment to draw out her flickers of inner wisdom. Still, the three of us knew she required far-improved care over what was possible in their residence no matter how well-meaning were her daily caregivers.

I (especially) needed to stand up to my father no matter his blustering reaction to being called on the carpet for his self-centered attitudes. Had I done so, my Mom's final days may have seen less suffering.

Don't let this regrettable lesson happen to you.

Clarify

If I were to ask, how confident do you consistently feel as to whether you're getting accurate or complete information about your parents' true state of affairs, what would I discover? I thought so.

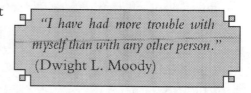

"I have had more trouble with myself than with any other person." (Dwight L. Moody)

You'd receive conflicting reports depending on what day of the week – sometimes what hour or minute – you ask!

You garner only the content one (typically the bossy partner) or both want you to know (when they collude). Never more accurate than during the episode we shall aptly entitle "The Driving Test"... For an addendum, see the section on auto insurance renewal within My Story.

This tale dates to November 2010. All I know for a fact is this: Something happened between the first and fifth of that month. On November 1st, my father was due to undergo Ontario's bi-annual process for seniors over 80 years of age. This includes: attending a safety lecture with a qualified instructor; providing optometrist proof of a recent eye examination; and completing a multiple-choice written test to demonstrate supposed competence pertaining to the province's rules of the road.

Notably, demonstration of actual capability behind the wheel via a road driving test is not demanded in Ontario at the time of publication. It **should** be.

At any rate, when we chatted that Monday, I learned – to my initial horror – my father did not walk out with official papers signed, sealed and delivered – the way he'd done at ages 80, 82, 84 and 86. It's no hyperbole to state this was a shock to us both. For, despite all his braggart ways (more on this later), he could justifiably claim a stellar record across 72 or so previous years.

To this day, I have yet to discern what exactly unfolded across the next four days. All I know is that by the Friday, he had signed papers in hand. What the H--- had happened in the meantime??

Knowing my Dad as I do, I can only surmise a few possibilities: 1) He flubbed the written test; or 2) He was kicked out of the lecture. I rule out not having the appropriate optometrist paperwork, for that is something he would've diligently looked after around the time of "The Missing Glasses Episode".

Why I zoom in on the two theories is this:

a. He would **never** permit me or him, for that matter, to hold anything but the most arrogant opinion of his driving prowess. To describe him as anything less than "Bill the [summer] Truck Driver who (in his imagination) single-handedly won WWII by driving engine mounts to the plant manufacturing Lancaster Bombers of WWII Fame" would destroy his ego beyond recognition. I'm not joking concerning how he thinks of himself.

b. As adamant as he remains that he's got *"a thing or two to teach that guy about driving who doesn't even own a vehicle for Pete's sake"*, I can readily envision my father becoming so incensed at having to submit a fifth time to a mandatory lecture (which he stridently believes totally beneath his dignity and only necessary for unworthy peons) that he was expelled from class!

Back to **Laughter** as a means to right-size otherwise completely exasperating circumstances, do you permit me and Derek the total roar we had over a retired school principal being thrown out of the room for belligerence? That one was good for about fifteen minutes of straight belly laughs!!

At any rate, back to my theme…Short of monitoring them 24 hours a day – which we've already established you're not prepared to do for your Un-cope-able Parents – some ability to clarify what's **really** going on is called for.

This requires the sleuthing skills of the finest detective! You need intelligence. This means asking what types of questions? That's right! Think back on all those communication skills training programs you've attended on open-ended questions. And plenty of them to boot!

Notice how **Neutrality** (so that your buttons don't get pushed by what you hear) and **Openness** (to allow you to take in the full picture) will come in exceptionally handy when you **Clarify**. Do you start to see how **Being** and **Doing** go hand-in-hand?

P.S. As a bridge into the actions of **Trust** and **Observe**, I determined through careful listening and focused questions that the most likely explanation regarding the failed driving test was…flunking the exam. Why? Too many phone calls leading up to "The Big Day" had been devoted to talking about studying for the written portion without supporting evidence said preparation was actually taking place. Even though we don't have children ourselves, donning my Sherlock Holmes hat inspired the intuition he was trying to pull the wool over my eyes. Like any kid worth their salt would on an unsuspecting parent! Chastised by the instructor, he pulled several all-nighters in a row that resulted in a passing grade by Friday. The little devil!!

Trust

To quote a number of writers in the spirituality field, it is said each of us designed a blueprint for our time on Earth that includes the lessons we're here to absorb plus the challenges we're meant to forge past. These authors purport that we choose every one and every thing in our lives.

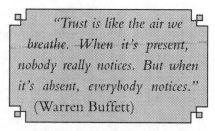

"*Trust is like the air we breathe. When it's present, nobody really notices. But when it's absent, everybody notices.*"
(Warren Buffett)

No matter how intensely nerve-wracking I've found my father and mother across the decades, I oddly don't balk at the idea I selected both from the countless available options on the Planet before my arrival. Why those two?? Well, don't think I haven't asked myself that question on more than one occasion!!

Seriously, though, when I reframe my upsets into a willing decision made from a higher plane, it somehow elevates my broader comprehension of our lives together. I don't diminish the adversity experienced at their hands. Yet, I appreciate I ultimately emerged stronger for having endured those hardships.

Going further, I embrace the notion that my parents chose one another in marriage to bring forth their own series of trials and tribulations. This soul contract was part of their individual plus shared journeys. Here's how their unwritten 'paperwork' read:

- (Mother) You will please give me a roof over my head, provide for us and impregnate me with a child.
- (Father) I agree to do those things and in return you will be my house-slave (notice I did not even say housewife) to your dying day.

Yes, I realize how hard-nosed this assessment sounds. Nonetheless, if you knew my parents – and few now do – you'd agree it's 1,000% true.

From this detached perspective (even if my words don't sound it), I find calming surety that affords me faith to know all has been unfolding as fated.

Jerry and Esther Hicks would say my parents showed me contrast on several levels. Contrast, in their terms, refers to behaviors or attitudes we find objectionable in others. Without contrast, these Vortex authors propose we wouldn't know ourselves.

I've indeed found this true with my parents. Through their often-ungracious and mostly-unconscious demeanor, they indirectly embedded in me a fundamental commitment toward nobility of carriage and deep self-awareness.

While honoring what's good in your folks, the contrast they offer lets you decide what's right by you – perhaps even their opposite.

If we re-consult Martha Beck's breakthrough article, loving detachment would give rise to easy acceptance of soul contracts like the one existent between my folks across 50-plus years of marriage. When I look from that vantage point, it is clear both had agreed she'd stay in their home until her last breath. They shared high needs for familiarity and security – likely borne of their Depression-era upbringing.

I'd go so far as to say – using my shrewd instinctive powers – that their compact included living until 90. My mother made it to her 90th year, which was good enough. My father holds on during his 90th year. Any time now, it would be entirely possible if he were to decide to rejoin her in Heaven. Contract fulfilled. (I'm sure you know of many an enduring marriage where one partner passed within a short period of the other.)

Strangers looking in on my Mom's final days would see a chaotic zoo. Yet, it's equally possible from a 30,000 foot view to come up with an entirely different interpretation. Beneath choppy seas lie still waters.

If all else fails, have you ever tried the pose of an Alien visiting our solar system? I'm sure they would simply 'smile' in recognition of how curious these Earthlings appear to be.

Initiate

No matter how abhorrent it may feel to intervene in the best interests of one or both parents, I'm here – unfortunately – to let you know you're going to have to. In My Story, I deal with this facet further.

> "*Vow that you will never again please anyone so that he or she will be pleased with you. Succeed in this and you will hear another chain drop.*" (Vernon Howard)

For now, suffice to say my folks had so worn me out by my mid-20's, I hoped beyond all hope that might be it for the balance of my life and theirs. Like maybe, by some miracle of miracles, they'd comport their elder years with dignity. What galaxy was I part of?? They'd rarely been composed of that fabric in their young years. Why would it change all of a sudden as they grew old? If anything, worse!

So, if you're waiting for some explicit invitation to rescue them, you're going to linger forever. Unluckily, it's your lot to dredge up every remaining shred of courage and perseverance to go back in there one last time to *"Git 'er done"*.

Of course, my allusions to finality are loosely-based. In that, we all know this is going to be a (long) series of interventions. Don't we?

By definition, Un-cope-able Parents can't be handled in one sitting. If you genuinely believed this, I'm sorry to burst your bubble.

That's why I devoted so much attention to the **LOVING** qualities of **Laughter, Openness, Vibration, Intention, Neutrality and Grace**. They'll be your salvation as you undertake some possibly loathsome tasks.

Because, you realize – don't you? – Un-cope-able Parents will fight you *every* step of the way! God almighty! If you're the least bit wishy-washy, you're doomed.

Borrowing from my infinite arsenal of personal elder stories, do you have any concept of how **often** I tried to contribute in their household during the phase when my mother's hips… cataracts… bladder… arthritis…and…and…and… made it increasingly impossible to sustain her house-slave duties? Do you have any theories as to the response I got? You're correct! I was rebuffed by my father at every turn. Ironically, on those occasions I put my foot down, he was pleased as punch over leaving in my wake a freshly-cleaned household from top to bottom. Go figure.

Since my Mom passed away, Initiation has been considerably easier – on my Dad. Not so much on me…

As a consequence, I've learned something about timing in this equation. What was once off-limits in the performance of daughterly support has slowly transformed into the accepted norm.

Overwhelmed by the indeed-daunting stacks of papers…and objects…and cleaning…and sorting…and…and…and… that had slowly accumulated over a decade, my father was now only too grateful to allow me complete access into those farthest reaches room-by-room to wrest back some semblance of organization from the disastrous mess. I thus measure my progress these days in millimeters. Even a small corner tamed is great cause for jubilant celebration!

Yes, I'm still subject at a moment's notice to one of my Dad's famous hollered lines: *"Don't touch my stuff!!"* He means his piles… and piles…and piles… littered across every available surface of the downstairs where he basically cloisters. The phrase is practically a mantra, over which my husband and I just shake our heads. I've learned to ignore it.

Instead, like a General strategically executing the intricacies of his battle campaign, my father's daughter is stealthily encroaching on his territory inch my inch. You better believe I shall be triumphant in gaining order over his very bunker itself! (This term was appropriately assigned by my cousin whom I sincerely thank for its WWII accuracy.)

All the while, my father's feedback on the work is prideful. His thankfulness is sincere. We have arrived at a partnership of sorts over time.

Observe

By observe, I mean applying any
and all finely-honed powers of
observation you've developed to
date:

> *"While you were busy judging others you left your closet open and your skeletons fell out."*
> (Anonymous)

- Listening for what's not
  being said just as much, if
  not more, than what is being spoken;
- Watching body language, like the art I developed as a
  teenager to notice the nanosecond twitch of my father's eye
  to discern when he's uncomfortable or downright lying;
- Noticing verbal "trucs" (French for tricks) like blustering
  and argumentativeness when he wants to throw others off
  his trail (this one used to work beautifully on my intimidated
  mother, but it doesn't thwart me because I've learned to
  circumnavigate it);
- Picking up on a doubtful hemming-and-hawing tone he
  displays when I've caught him red-handed in an act of
  subterfuge.

You parents out there – draw upon your instincts in watching out for
your children and teenagers. Don't you need hawk-like observational
skills and animal-like listening acuity to sniff out any game-playing,
deceit or avoidance tactics? You have a distinct advantage over childless
people like me who must rely on our equivalent talents sharpened in
business and elsewhere.

Nonetheless, we all have our means by which we're able to read our
parents' every facial expression and movement.

If nothing else, haul out the resources you developed as a child to
gauge how far you could stretch the envelope of manipulation to get

your way with Mom and Dad! Or, perhaps it's more apropos to take you back to teen-hood when you had to sneak past curfew on a hot date.

Either way, I think you'll concur that your powers of **Observation** become indispensable alongside the **Clarifying** questions you ask. This potent combination will either confirm or disprove your gut about what's really going on.

Are you ready for another short story? This one is named "The Stolen Garage Door Opener".

Just when everything was going along peacefully in the household – Bam! Another emergency hit. In 2010, crisis arrived in the form of my father locking himself out during the scattered week (as it turned out) leading up to my mother's transition. In 2011, that same disarrayed dynamic (interestingly around the 1-year anniversary) led to a wholesale replacement of the garage door system.

Boy, oh boy. Due to several closely-spaced vehicular mishaps (you'll find an expanded version in My Story), my father had just received back from the auto dealership his two (!) repaired cars. I stand firm to this day that the former door opener will be found in one of these two places: 1) Underneath a floor mat or wedged within the passenger seat of his 1987 Cutlass; or 2) Lost in the morass of his endless junk in the basement!

Do you want to know my Dad's ingrained theory? He refuses to be swayed.

He will argue you into the ground if you suggest anything other than the idea, the woman delivering his mail for a period of time somehow broke through the front door (he keeps it neurotically locked day and night), immediately found the old device on a littered bench in the hall and stole it with the objective of creeping back during the dark to commit who-knows-what nefarious acts in his garage!

Unhappily, the case for logic is not aided by the fact she was apparently nowhere to be found on the postal route several weeks later or since! *"Aha, I was right all along"*, my father chortled. *"They must have uncovered her scheme and summarily dismissed her."*

Trust me. At this point it will be when my father passes and I'm going through his last effects that I'll locate the missing device, proving one of my suspicions accurate.

In the meantime, he incurred unnecessary expense plus aggravation in the installation of a *"new-fangled"* system which makes him more petrified to operate than reassured. To put icing on the cake, he also replaced anew the entire front-door lock that had only been installed the previous spring! Oh, my God. All these costly and needless decisions rendered without a drop of consultation – despite the fact we speak virtually every day... A fait accompli before I could utter one syllable of sense...

I should think "The Stolen Garage Door Opener" incident demonstrates there comes a moment when you can no longer accept at face value anything they say – no matter how vociferously your sneaky elders would attempt to dissuade you otherwise.

I reiterate: The capacity to see through their oft-unsophisticated games with **Laughter** will help you maintain a level head.

As I regularly express with my contemporaries: *"Surely they must recognize we see through their thinly-disguised veneer. Don't they?"* [heads moving side to side in a "no"] *"They must be deluded that we're not adults in our own right but still think of us as five years of age!"* [nodding heads]

Apparently!

iNnovate

OK, so I 'cheated' on this last of the ACTION acronym! I sought a word that captured the requirement for novel approaches to cope with Un-cope-able Parents.

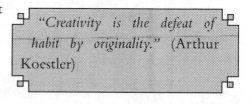

"Creativity is the defeat of habit by originality." (Arthur Koestler)

Innovation is it. With its connotation of novelty and originality, innovation perfectly expresses how out-of-the-box your solutions need to be in order to stay a step ahead (at minimum) of your crafty elders!

Just as standard answers don't work for the truly impossible, so too don't any of the negative A to Z formulas you may have experimented with in the past.

Now, at first blush, the following (positive) A to Z list may strike you as somewhat juvenile. I hear you. On other hand, haven't you already tried all the unreasonable tactics? How far did they get you? Not very!

Thus, like the astute Mother Superior in *The Sound of Music* (film) counsels Sisters frantically searching for Maria within the abbey, I'd suggest you look in the *un*familiar places for cleverness that brings you tangible results with your aging folks.

This will entail setting aside your agendas – hidden and otherwise – regarding what *you'd* prefer to do. Instead, I call you forth to rise up to **be** and **do** what will serve your parents' greatest interests.

Here we go. Prepare to receive your A to Z compendium of what **does** work.

- Acknowledgement (of their inner Essence)
- Balance (maintain your own center through it all)
- Compassion

- Determination
- Empathy
- Focus
- Gentleness
- Hope (keep up the faith!)
- Ingenuity
- Joking (not at their expense, but offering almost a sense of playfulness)
- Kindness
- Listening
- Mastery (of self)
- Nurturing
- Optimism
- Patience
- Questioning (in the positive sense of showing sincere interest)
- Respect
- Stamina
- Thankfulness (for what they sacrificed on your behalf)
- Understanding
- Vulnerability (not as a psychological ruse but rather as tenderness)
- Wisdom
- X-treme self-care
- Yearning (to ease their burden)
- Zen (calmness)

When you scan down this list of qualities and attitudes, do you notice anything? If you answered how "soft" most of the attributes seem, you win the prize!

This is quite purposeful on my part.

At last, the scales of corporate justice (ever-so-slowly) begin to favor those leaders and organizations high on Emotional Intelligence instruments in their quest to attract, retain and engage the next-generation workforce. In a similar vein concerning Un-cope-able

Parents, I offer a reminder of what my friend, Suzette, drummed into me years ago: *"You catch more flies with honey than vinegar."*

Wow, did I inwardly rebel when she trotted out that catch-phrase! But she's right.

When all is said and done, we've established your Real Self genuinely longs to support your aging folks with kindness so they and you can go to your graves certain you did everything in your capability for them.

Since that is your heartfelt **Intention**, I respectfully submit under **iNnovate** my very best thinking on this subject to-date.

Besides, wasn't it Einstein who said: *"The problems of tomorrow cannot be solved at the same level of thinking that created them in the first place"*? How valid! You've already experimented – like Edison discovering 9,999 ways how not to create a light bulb – with every technique that doesn't work.

Are you (finally) through with banging your head against the wall? Excellent!!

Then how about giving these alternative **ACTION** verbs a try?

Question & Answer Time!

Were you wondering when we'd get to some insights concerning the Impossible Parents Questionnaire? Here we are!

Beyond the two Keys to Coping of LOVING ACTION…and besides the wisdom that follows where others share their experiences…may I offer these additional pointers to help guide your Un-cope-able Parents journey?

Question #1: Your eyeballs roll into the farthest reaches of your head at the mere thought of them.

While understandable, this is purely a chosen thought pattern. It can be changed. I recommend you do so. For, if you allow merely the thought of your parents to victimize you to that extent, you're going to be in deep trouble long before you enter their company. May I suggest instead that you concentrate upon all the things you **appreciate** about them? Remember: What we focus upon expands. Think unwanted thoughts and you'll get more of them.

Question #2: You have to spend hours "psyching" yourself up while getting ready to be in their presence.

Rather than "psyching" up, I recommend you define readiness as preparation. Like eyeball-rolling, the former connotes Poor Me, whereas the latter is an adult stance. Just as you're a proactive professional at work, so too in your dealings with loved ones. I'm all for techniques borrowed from my Reiki practice like grounding myself by imagining roots growing out my feet as well as forming an invisible protective bubble around my energetic aura.

Question #3: You want to tear out your hair strand by strand before, during and/or after interacting with them (even if have a full head of hair, you'd never possess enough for all you'd like to yank).

Within the notion of "want to" lies an equivalent sentiment – "feel like". Whenever I hear that phrase ("feel like" tearing out my hair) from coaching clients, my ears perk up. For, it marks evidence of an **old belief system** in operation. Programmed as you may be, you yet possess the ability to release tired scripts. What messages are you telling yourself in those moments? How is it serving you to keep repeating them? Reframe and stay calm!

Question #4: You grind your teeth to their roots while clamping down on what you'd really wish with all your might to say – and that's just in one phone call!

Careful! If you're giving over your attention to what you want to say, you may miss some important data along the way. You know how stealthy your folks can get. As I regularly reassure participants in my communication skills programs, you won't forget your points by the time the other person finishes their sentence. This is a typical concern. It accounts for: interrupting the other; drawing false assumptions; and myriad bad habits. **Listen** first and then speak!

Question #5: You risk at any moment to lose all your accumulated knowledge, wisdom, experience and skill because they manage (for the millionth time) to destroy your capability due to their attitudes, beliefs or actions.

This one is an unfounded fear. You know what **FEAR** stands for: False Evidence Appearing Real. No one can pinch you off from the competent person you are without your permission. Are you allowing your folks to shrink you into that still-small child within? Stop it! You're granting them too much power. You're in command. If anything, they need the parenting. Like infants, you must be present to their needs (without sacrificing your own).

Question #6: You have to endure hours-long diatribes having nothing to do with the immediate subject matter at hand in order to wait to make your key points with one or both folks.

Derek coined the bang on phrase, *"Did I tell you...well, anyway...* I'm hooting! It's when we're both subjected to a story for the zillionth time (and want to scream) – especially when he rarely asks if we'd heard it and we respond in unison with a resounding *"Yes!!"* March right on, Pa... You see, without his **story**, he has no identity. He needs to endlessly recite his glory days as a means of drawing life-force. We shut it out and let him drone on.

Question #7: You are completely spent – physically, emotionally, mentally and spiritually – on the heels of spending time with them (it doesn't matter whether this is hours or minutes).

Time for some **"extreme self-care"**! Note: This does not equate to selfish!! The metaphor is akin to donning your own oxygen mask first in an airline emergency. Eldercare is unequivocally draining. That's why you need to pay special attention to self-nurturing during this exceptionally wit-testing life phase. What brings you pleasure? Do it! For me, it's leisurely bubble baths. Place boundaries around visits; don't bite off more than can be chewed at one time.

Question #8: You have to demonstrate Super-Human powers of perseverance, endurance, patience and fortitude in order to prevail.

To countermand the unattractive doggedness we adult children can fall into as part of an obsession to achieve our opinionated outcomes around aging parents, let me enumerate Martha Beck's three steps (refer back to "Neutrality"):

      a. Identify what (your father or mother) must change to make you happy. This involves thinking about how your loved one must alter their self before you can be content. Elaborate how you'd feel if the change occurred.

    b. Next, remove everything but how you'd feel.

    c. Finally, shift your focus from controlling your loved one's behavior to creating your own happiness. This is the moment you become mentally free to start trying innovative ideas and lift up from the hopeless deadlock of depending on change from someone you can't manipulate anyway.

Question #9: You know in the deepest places of your interior what is called for in their situation and they will have none of it.

Don't give up! What might seem impossible to resolve at one point in time can suddenly break through wondrously in another moment. Evidence my father's earlier obstinacy on the cleaning front. They don't say patience is a heavenly trait for nothing! Remember: Everything on this Earth plane unfolds according to Divine Timing. Often, like pieces of a jigsaw puzzle, certain elements must fall into place before others come to fruition. Don't rush the **sequence**.

Question #10: You feel you've attempted every available device known to mankind and yet you make zero headway in influencing them to see your point of view.

May I quote from Doreen Virtue's guidebook to *Healing with the Angels: Oracle Cards* to address this concern? "Surrender & Release" is the perfect message! When you hold on tightly to a part of your life that's not working, it has no room to heal. However, if you're willing to open your hands and allow it to be freed, one of two situations will occur: Either it will be washed away from you or the issue will heal in a miraculous way. Try not to control the outcome of your troubling situation. **Let go** and let the Universe help you.

YOU'RE NOT ALONE ANYMORE

As with so many beliefs formerly held over the past half-century, I've done a 360-degree about-face concerning my perceived uniqueness of living with Un-cope-able Parents. As if I'm the only

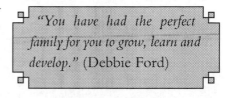
"You have had the perfect family for you to grow, learn and develop." (Debbie Ford)

person on the globe dealing with almost-impossible elder dynamics... Not so!

That's why the 2010 Staff Room dialogue with those teachers was so powerful and meaningful.

It's like when I found out – to my sheer amazement at the time – I'm not the only child who grew up in a dysfunctional alcoholic (paternal) and mentally-ill (maternal) environment. Far from it!

Still, it hit me between the eyes when I discovered that those ladies were yanking out their hair as I was. Paradoxically, what a relief!! No longer did I feel alone in the world. You have no idea what a strange gratitude that was. Like an Atlas-burden had been lifted from my shoulders...

As a consequence, *Coping with Un-cope-able Parents* is my first publication where I've deliberately sought others' perspectives who are withstanding similar situations – to enhance your reading experience. My hope in so doing is that you'll uncover additional enlightenment through the varying scenarios these friends and colleagues bring to the table.

You've heard plenty enough of my examples! And, there's more to come in My Story!

So, how about we now turn to other voices so they can reveal their truth with you… I know I found bearing witness to their tales a fascinating experience in its own right. I have no doubt you will, too!

When the Parental Home Becomes Too Much

Background

Nine years after my father passed away, it was becoming clear that managing the house in which my parents had lived for 47 years was becoming too much for my overwhelmed mother.

The Challenge

However, fear of change and the unknown – coupled with perceived security in the familiar – resulted in great reluctance to let go of the family home. It was like her identity. Her possessions were seen as parts of her. All my Mom's memories were in that house, as she reflected upon having built it with my Dad. She truly believed on a certain level that if she abandoned their residence, it would be like minimizing or even disrespecting the remembrance of her beloved spouse.

Recommended Tactics

What really shifted my Mom's willingness to overcome her worries about entering a retirement residence (i.e. perceived loss of freedom and independence, fear of how to deal with the unexpected, questions about whether she'll even like it there) was taking her to lunch with a friend's mother. She had to see the place for herself. Like all of us, she'd heard the maltreatment horror stories. At minimum, she lacked confidence in her ability to be there on her own. At worst, her underlying fear was, *"what will happen to me when my children leave me here?"* Once someone her own age showed my Mom around and her peers chatted socially, she was like a duck in water! *"Been there, done it"* describes her attitude these days.

Lessons Learned

For the elderly, it's all about their comfort zone. You just need to accept they're set in their mannerisms. As such, your suggestions in no way, shape or form can hint of threat. Otherwise, they'll become insecure and likely fight you every step of the way. Forcing them absolutely does not work!

Go Near at Your Own Risk

Background

My mother (a term I use loosely) is a delusional and severely-obese woman who's had a narcissistic personality disorder since her 20's; she's now 75. A self anointed martyr and overly-emotional, everything is always about her. She blames me as the sole cause for her "great romantic" husband abandoning us. To help her "recover" from the divorce, she was sent off to Europe for four years while I lived with her parents, and as a toddler I was returned to her "care" when she got back.

The Challenge

It shouldn't prove much of a stretch to imagine that this situation - abandoned by a father and enduring a broken mother - inflicted damage to my spirit at an early age. Even today at age 55, I feel I continue to pay a high price for what happened so many years ago. I'm single and conflicted about a committed, long term female relationship. I have the ability to enjoy deep lasting friendships, however. Five years ago (partially against my better instincts), I enlisted my healthiest and most-trusted friend to visit her home state. Given her apparent conversion to born-again Christianity, we thought it safe to attend church together. What were we thinking?? What enemy – never mind mother – would be such a vacuum cleaner of hope (the Devil incarnate) to look me in the eye and say: *"I predict you will lose your salvation"*. I turned pale, then white with anger and removed myself from that visit quickly. That sword-thrust of a statement for me serves as the crowning confirmation of her truly-evil state.

Recommended Tactics

As a consequence of her emotional violation, I kept my mother at arm's length for about five years after that disastrous visit. No engagement. Like a dangerously-hot stove, don't go near – no matter what! Only last year, out of some pity for her age and economic situation did I begin to send her gift cards (but not dollars) to supplement her often-dire finances. Surprisingly, she has respected my boundaries and sends thank-you notes and cards. She seems genuinely thankful and humbled, but I still keep her at arm's length, convinced of her toxicity. I support her not out of guilt or with expectation, but because I choose to. Nonetheless, the idea of an in-person visit remains unpalatable. My personal boundaries are strong and clear. I am considering a phone call once or twice a year, but am conflicted about this.

Lessons Learned

To this day, I can become very angry about what my mother has – or more accurately has not – done over the years. I recognize I have many unresolved wounds. Unduly hard on myself, I consistently examine where I may be at fault. Year over year, I'm learning not to give over my power to others in "automatic-Child mode" but instead to stay in my Adult. It helps that my brother – the enabler and favorite – has now woken up to her games. In the end, it's about my own healing, I therefore also believe it's OK to wish my mother would simply pass away quietly and quickly. I accord myself that freedom.

In Denial

Background

My mother is 73 years old and suffering from Alzheimer's. She was diagnosed three years ago. My father is 81 and was recently diagnosed with the mixed dementia of Alzheimer's and vascular disease. Anyone contending with these terrible afflictions knows one effect is that normal conversational "filters" progressively disappear. As such, what gets declared in anger or upset must be taken with the proverbial grain of salt.

The Challenge

Always prideful in her spotless housekeeping standards, my mother's ability to maintain cleaning, cooking and other traditional duties has naturally seen serious decline in recent years. It has been extremely sad to watch. My sibling and I tried to "pick up the slack" for some while in order to safeguard her dignity. That is, until it eventually got to be too much, what with full-time jobs and young families of our own.

Recommended Tactics

To our credit, we recognized that something had to be done about our parents' deteriorating household. We basically issued an "ultimatum" – declaring that if they want to stay in their home (which they do), they must accept housekeeping support from a hired resource. All well and good! However, we didn't bargain on my mother being convinced the domestic worker had stolen her jeans when she couldn't locate them – even though the sizing was completely off. In her re-telling of events she accused my wife's mother of coming to the house to clean and then going upstairs to her bedroom where my mother-in-law reportedly took and walked out with them under her arms. My mother proceeded to tell her older sister; born only 15 months' apart and always close, my aunt found it hard to believe such a story. She called my sister to clarify matters. Eventually my sister phoned and told me what had transpired. When I talked to my father, I couldn't believe that he agreed with my mother's story. Heads at first bashing against the wall! That's why I agree whole-heartedly with your suggestions to apply clarity and humor to these challenging circumstances. We really had to probe to get to the bottom of the matter while finding ways to stay calm ourselves.

Lessons Learned

In 20/20 hindsight, my sibling and I should have been more aware of these changes happening in the moment. We recommend to others in a similar situation to watch for early indicators like the fact that my father's view of "reality" is now different. For instance, when we asked Papa if he really believed the clothing lies, he shrugged: *"It could happen…"* When we furthered with: *"You know Mama has Alzheimer's which means she can't remember"*, he retorted: *"I no believe"*. That is when we realized his judgment was becoming skewed as well. In hindsight, this was the eventual beginning of our role of becoming parents to our parents.

SURVIVING & TRANSFORMING THE ABUSE

Background

My sister and I were emotionally and verbally abused as children by our mother. For me, alone as far as I know, there was also an incident of overt sexual abuse when I was twelve, disguised as medical assistance and capping off years of invasive physical touching. My mother has always been a narcissistic and manipulative person with many vices including lying. We call her the Pink Elephant in the middle of our family living room.

The Challenge

"Where does one begin?" Of course it all should have been handled differently years ago; but it wasn't. This is reality. In fact, four decades later while multiple pachyderm obstacles have been scaled, our family dysfunction remains firmly in place. My sibling and I share only one goal: access to my father. He has always been the altruistic and loving parent, befuddled by my antipathy toward my mother. He is enabling and co-dependent upon his wife. If I want to enjoy even a diminished relationship with my father, I must keep the illusion of one with my mother.

Recommended Tactics

I learned relatively recently from my mother's youngest sister that they were both sexually abused for years by their father. While I have forgiven my mother for passing along that legacy, I do not love or even like her. Forgiveness will have to be enough. As a result, I try to be a less angry version of my teenage self and have, occasionally, mustered a modicum of maturity. But I have found far greater success from an unexpected source, much smaller yet mightier than any elephant: my delightful little dog. I made a conscious decision to not have children, and admit my own childhood played no small part in this outcome. So Molly, unwittingly, has become a surrogate grandchild for my parents, one with whom my mother *can* enjoy a relationship. My father derives much joy from taking her on endless walks and doling out on-demand tummy rubs. I have, finally, discovered a way to be a daughter-like presence in their home, yet with sanity-inducing distance. My dog, quite frankly, allows me to honor my parents. And that will have to be enough.

Lessons Learned

I don't know that I'm recommending this as a tactic, and I definitely would not advise offering up a real grandchild to fill this gap. Where our family is at today is best summarized by my father who said, *"Molly's been good for us."* And really, my parents are both in their eighties; how much longer can this last?

TIME TO SURRENDER THE CAR KEYS

Background

My mother and father have been together for 45 years. Most assuredly, they've developed their own "systems" with one other – even if not entirely comprehensible or logical to us as their children. Whether right or wrong, my father over-relies on my mother to carry around *their* important documents and items (e.g. bank book, keys, eye glasses) in *her* purse. Their long-standing dependent arrangement is posing escalating problems, as she continues to lose her own capabilities.

The Challenge

An instance of the latter is that my mother had to go out in bad weather around Easter; driving conditions were icy. She hit another vehicle two kilometers from home and didn't tell anyone! Somehow, she and my father managed to get the car to a nearby body shop for secretive repair. Then, she promptly parked the fixed auto in her garage and "forgot" about the matter! The only thing is, someone followed her home and reported the incident to Police. We became aware when we went over for a visit and reviewed a letter she had received outlining the incident.

Recommended Tactics

Having skirted a near-disaster, my siblings and I stepped up our active involvement in our parents' affairs. While we cannot be on-site 24 X 7, we found ways to better share our responsibilities around continuous check-ins so no one singularly bears the burden. (For only children, I suggest reaching out for similar support to trusted friends and family members.)

Lessons Learned

This potentially-lethal "judgment call" on my mother's part could have had wide-ranging consequences had she injured someone (or worse). I don't even want to think! It really points out the consequences of letting our parents make critical decisions for themselves once they are beyond a certain point. It's vital to know when to take away car keys and/or other privileges. Save them from themselves! In hindsight, this was an early sign she was undergoing cognitive changes which was impacting her judgment.

FAKE DRAMAS

Background

My mother is 80 years old and has been feigning ill-health for half her life. She's actually in excellent health, save some osteoporosis. The "whys" don't matter to me. Not anymore! It's enough to know many people like this exist and I'm the frustrated daughter of one of them.

The Challenge

My mother enjoys using these vague and non-specific ailments to play Lady-of-the-Manor while trying to engage her husband and adult children in the roles of personal servants. She vies for a share of the attention that should deservedly go to those actually in ill-health who often avoid taking to their sick beds so as to live life to the fullest. My mother's act has actually included three death-bed scenes to date. Like Lazarus, she miraculously rises a few days later (to catch-up on her TV programs, unlike Lazarus who was born-died-reborn long before this medium). While tempted to call out "Brava" during these performances, more often than not one has to concentrate to hold in rightful temper in the face of such a farce.

Recommended Tactics

Her ruse sometimes works on the butler – I mean my father. My sister, brother-in-law and I, however, refuse to take direction and must prove a tremendous disappointment to the playwright. Instead, I assume the role of audience versus cast member reluctantly attending a very bad and repetitive theatre bit that should have been cancelled long ago. I also see myself as a fellow drama critic along with my sibling and her husband. We compare notes to share our frustrations and use our senses of humor to recount the funniest bits. We mostly exit stage left before the final curtain call.

Lessons Learned

Get your hands on some good theatre tickets. The End.

ACCEPTING IT'S OK TO BE LOOKED AFTER

Background

My father passed away at age 67 in 1984. This was quite soon after both my parents retired and moved to their ideal setting. My mother, a former teacher who had worked hard all her life, was devastated. To her, all their dreams of retirement had ended. She had been quite dependent on my father. He drove her everywhere and looked after the banking. With my siblings' help, she obtained her driver's license and took control of her finances. From the time of my father's death, she really didn't live alone – enjoying the benefits of living with one of her children or right next door. For about 20 years, everything pretty much worked out. My mother seemed content – considering the circumstances. As she reached her mid-80's, my sister found living next door to her quite challenging; she could no longer drive and became 'house bound' on the farm. My sibling and her family had busy lives and couldn't always take her with them. They became worried about leaving her alone and she, in turn, became lonely.

The Challenge

A wanderer at heart, my mother never feared change. She loved going out and, if affordable, taking the odd trip. She was also very generous with her money – despite living from check to check on a small teacher's pension. Even though she helped out my sister's family and other nieces and nephews, it became clear she couldn't continue to live with them. My brother found a beautiful assisted-living complex where she could keep her independence at only a 5 to 10 minute walk from his house. At first looking forward to it, she changed her mind once moved in. She kept talking about moving back to her mobile home or into an inexpensive apartment. After many discussions, it became apparent she was worried about money. She had to pay rent to live in her unit, but all needs (including meals) were taken care of and she had some spending money for small extra things. Used to helping others, she couldn't reconcile herself to not being able to do this anymore. Her pension checks were now used to look after her needs. She felt guilty about this as well as the fact that her place was so nice.

Recommended Tactics

We needed to convince her to stay where she was as it really did meet all her needs except for financially helping others. All her seven children were in agreement with the strategy of discussing the following:

- The ongoing costs of living in a private apartment (electricity, phone, cable, furnishings, food etc.) would be more expensive and, therefore, would leave her with her with even less money.

- She had companionship where she was living. If she moved to her own apartment she would be alone for the most part.

- She had worked hard all her life and struggled to provide for us. She deserved to sit back and be looked after for once. We were all successful. Nieces and nephews were well provided for. There was no need to feel guilty about not helping out.

- What really turned things around was when we talked about our peace of mind. When she was in the retirement home, we didn't worry about her. We knew she was well attended to and we enjoyed visiting her in such lovely surroundings. During her life, she always put her children first. Telling her how it made us feel sealed the deal. When she realized it made us happy, she saw the benefits in staying put.

- We also talked about how she could help out in the retirement residence. Since she was still so sharp she could make a difference by supporting those residents who needed some assistance to make their lives happier.

My mother is 93 now and seems very happy where she is. She has her wits about her and helps others adjust when they first arrive. My brother's family sees her just about every day. We all make a point of visiting her as often as we can, spread out as we are across the country. Not that she ever worried about this – she definitely doesn't feel abandoned.

Lessons Learned

It's important to find out what really worries the elderly when a change of this magnitude is presented. You must dig down to the core of what worries them and listen – really listen. They don't want to lose what's important to them. Once you fully understand that, it's a matter of coming up with a strategy that answers their concerns. Get them to think things through. If you have the right answers, they'll most likely accept the change. They must accept it without you forcing them – or it will not work.

THE ORDEALS OF CHRISTMAS SHOPPING

Background

In November every year I tell my parents (both healthy and in their 80s) that I am happy to do their Christmas shopping for them, but that orders will not be accepted after December 1st. I do this in the hopes they'll at least be done thinking of things that need buying by the week before Christmas. I'm not enamoured of shopping malls or crowds of any kind.

The Challenge

Of course my plan never works. This, despite my many reminders at my father's mid-November birthday and my phone check-ins every few days in December... I ask *"Any more purchases you'd like me to make?"* – my adult equivalent of the child-question, *"Are we there yet?"*. There are always last-minute requests. On occasion, these have included Christmas Eve. As my frustration rises, my Christmas cheer inversely declines.

Recommended Tactics

In a nutshell? Grin and bear it. Plus I schedule some time just in case, and when no *"sorry-to-bother-you-dears"* emerge, I've found time which I use not to shop but to bask in the solitary bliss of my home.

Lessons Learned

Merry Christmas! And remember to shop early.

PATIENCE, PATIENCE

Background

With both in-laws experiencing rapid decline in their health, it was apparent they were struggling with day-to-day tasks and unable to manage any major ones. At first, they attempted to cope with the speed of change on their own. But as the pace escalated, they knew in their heart of hearts they were losing the battle.

The Challenge

Clearly, my husband and I had to step in, as the situation was becoming untenable. This involved helping them to identify and accept the support they required. As with many others, our challenges were compounded by needing to gain commitment from his siblings. Not to mention that neither parent wanted to "give up" their independence. They wanted to maintain the power mentally, but physically had lost it. Where they were at one time able to assist one another with their mounting issues, this was no longer sustainable. Both were tired and scared. Finding common ground on how to best support them (along with who would provide said assistance) was most difficult.

Recommended Tactics

First off, we listened. Really listened… They needed to feel a measure of control in this devolving situation, which came from feeling heard. Only then could we move on to clarifying their needs by showing understanding of what they had stated. This led into analysis of what sets of solutions would best meet those declared needs, feeding those back and then taking appropriate action. Encourage other siblings to provide support if possible. We have become increasingly explicit in the latter regard; it now takes the form of spelling out specifically what we need help with in the form of *"it would be nice if you could make yourself available for"* on exact dates and times. These steps have allowed my in-laws to feel looked after, thus minimizing their fear of the unknown.

Lessons Learned

Help the aged feel they are being "heard" by keeping them up to date on what you are doing for them, and call them often to monitor the situation. They apparently forget easily. For example, no sooner had we taken steps to completely put in place a Meals on Wheels service, than we learned neither parent had actually placed the requisite call to make it happen! How frustrating to see all that effort potentially fall through the cracks. To ensure our attempts do not go for naught, we now follow-up diligently. While providing reassurance, we confirm they have literally followed through on paperwork and other initiatives. If not, we go over there personally to guarantee it! Patience is the name of the game we play to stay sane. Make sure you take ample time for yourself along the way.

Better Planning Was Needed

Background

My mother and father are 85, having brought four children into the world across 60 years of marriage. I am the oldest. One of my siblings is institutionalized and the other is deceased. This leaves my sister and me to watch over them. She is located approximately 3 hours' away and we reside on practically opposite sides of the country. For over 52 years, my folks have been living in the lovely and comfortable home my father has upgraded and maintained including a large yard. A Master of Education, he has taught prestigiously, not only in Canada but on other continents, and has supported worthy international educational and musical projects. My mother also worked in the school system. As pillars of their community, "appearances" count for them big-time. As with many couples married in the 1950's, he controls the money – and had the final say in much of the decision-making.

The Challenge

My mother is still sharp as a tack, though subject increasingly to osteoporosis and arthritis. My father is experiencing mounting challenges stemming from Parkinson's disease – making 'navigation' of their three-storey abode more and more challenging. While both continue to enjoy social activities with friends and family, it's becoming ever-more clear they 'shouldn't' be living in their home anymore. Much of their time is consumed with day-to-day living (meal preparation, hygiene, house-keeping, medical needs, etc.). Despite serious sight and hearing issues, my father remains stubbornly insistent upon driving. So much so that he recently managed to renew his license without any authority process in place to double-check his competence! Admittedly, loss of his license will short-circuit their independence. Still, it's of major concern to us that this was allowed to happen.

Recommended Tactics

Yes, we managed to hire an external resource to attend to their needs daily, but it's only a matter of time until a higher level of care will be required within their residence. Yes, we have neighbors keeping an eye on them, but we feel that some of those folks are understandably growing weary of the responsibility. My sister and I offer emotional support through regular phone calls, and we've each undertaken multiple trips to begin the grueling process of de-cluttering their vast accumulation of possessions collected across decades of travels and living in the same house for 52 years. My parents' names are near the top of a list to enter an assisted-living facility once a spot becomes available. Not an easy feat! Seeing us as mindful of their safety, my mother is more accepting of our overtures, though she's not fully ready to release the home in which they've lived happily for so long. My father is entirely resistant – being convinced a facility is where *"people go to die"* and instead preferring to be carted out of their house in a pine box. If I may be so bold!

Lessons Learned

While my sibling and I have done certain things well, in retrospect, I'm upset we didn't 'push' our parents harder a few years ago to engage in better planning for the inevitable. Had more proactive steps been taken then, we might not be faced with assisted-living as our only option today. Respectful, we left them to their own devices until the past few months. Even now, we recognize loving patience is needed to "plant seeds" in their best interests. We strive to maintain their dignity – recognizing the entire process is heart-breaking. Still, as members of the Sandwich Generation balancing the adventures of our three grown-up sons with the burdens of elderly parents, my wife and I have vowed we will down-size – much sooner than my parents! Even while next-steps aren't imminent in our 50's, we refuse to similarly overwhelm our children later in life. And, I give myself permission to vent: *"Goll darn it, why didn't my parents plan properly for this years' ago?"*

Believe In Yourself Even If "The Parentals" Don't

Background

I was a child born out of wedlock in a small town in Nova Scotia; 1959 might as well have been 1929 in the eyes of the community. I was whisked off to Ontario to live with my paternal grandfather and his new wife who tended me while my mother worked. After discovering I was being abused by her, my mother moved us both to the big city...Toronto. After five years there, she met and married her current husband and started to build a family. My two siblings were born in my early teen years and became the center of their attention leaving me to care for them and begin a life-long resentment that would build over the years.

The Challenge

All I ever wanted was to be accepted into the "nucleus" family but all I ever felt was rejection and never being good enough. While I strove to make something of myself (which I did), nothing was ever acknowledged or appreciated. It became clear I was the "black sheep" of the family even though my siblings haven't accomplished much with their lives. They continue to be unhappy but steadfast in their obligation to the family. The difficulty over the years has been to separate myself from the hurt that is inflicted on me whenever I am in their presence. After trying many tactics to show what a great person I was, the results have never changed. Thus, my own personal definition of insanity ensued. Establishing relationships with my siblings was a challenge as we were many years apart in age and distance as they lived in another city.

Recommended Tactics

For me, the best tactic has been self-care – inspired by my dear friends who have encouraged me to believe in myself through their love and respect. It's important to know that it's okay to have these feelings about your family as not every unit is like the Brady Bunch. Find peace within yourself for who you truly are. Share your love where it's appreciated and honored. Engage in positive relationships with friends and at work. Take time to savor the goodness in your life and don't let others' opinions dictate who you are in this world. Reach out to family members who do support you; you'll be surprised at how fulfilling that can be. There are those who understand you; embrace them and be your best self. And last, don't forget to spread the joy!

Lessons Learned

Believe in yourself and have the confidence to know you can do anything;

Know you have something powerful to share with the world;

Be kind to others; karma is great;

Find friends that are like "real" family and;

Buy a puppy...it is unconditional love.

THE POWER TO WAIT

Background

Before age 11, memories of my mother are few. Oh, she was there every day – cooking, cleaning, playing tennis or bowling, "networking" (my term) – but I wasn't particularly conscious of her. Like many precocious daughters, I was Daddy's girl during our 'happy', if impoverished, childhood. A brat where my mother was concerned, she favored my two younger brothers. Having been very dependent on my father in most aspects, she didn't handle their split well. She tried her best to adapt to working full-time again as a bank teller. When my sister ran away from home, I became the family's tacit head and my mother's reluctant helpmate. Although not a drinker, my mother's emotional dependency was indicative of severe depression and anxiety, un-diagnosed and un-treated. She would have crying jags on my shoulder night after night as we struggled to maintain a sense of normality for my brothers. My sister returned for visits with her boyfriend within months, and the sexual abuse began. I had no one to turn to. My mother was in no condition to notice. By fifteen, I'd survived a suicide attempt and numerous cries for help that largely went unheard. I got married just weeks before my sixteenth birthday.

The Challenge

Paradoxically, I've become my mother's primary caregiver. You see, I'm the "responsible" one. We all pretend Mum is completely independent, but recognize we're living a lie for her benefit. My mother's social life largely consists of casual acquaintances through local seniors' centers, where she'll play cards of an afternoon. She lives alone. She's lonely. She sleeps a lot, and watches television for company. She follows the media like a lemming, and cites Dr. Phil and Joyce Meyer as if they were experts whom she knows intimately. She has no pets. Her eating habits are consistent, if not particularly healthy.

My mother exists. She's alive, but doesn't have a life of her own. "Weary" as far back as I can remember, I used to comment she was practicing to be an "old lady" in her forties. I've known folks in their

90's with more youth in their hearts, more bounce in their steps and more lights on upstairs than my mother. I'm not saying that to be cruel, just stating an observation. She shut down her learning center decades ago – not that it was ever especially well developed. I believe one can *"teach an old dog new tricks"*. First, one has to motivate the dog to learn, though. I've never discovered what would motivate her to do so.

Mum now suffers from numerous health issues in her late seventies, few of which she truly understands. I accompany her on doctor's visits more frequently as she ages, trying to ensure she follows his recommendations and prescriptions. It's a lost cause as she rarely pays attention. She has become a crotchety and opinionated old woman.

It would be so easy to simply drop my mother from our lives – but not dutiful. Love is a powerful antidote if it exists, even dutiful love. I try to be present by being there physically and tending to her needs, especially in times of "crisis". Sometimes I make her day under the guise of companionship by stopping by unexpectedly and staying for a cup of tea, putting in a few pieces of a jigsaw puzzle or playing a game of King's Cribbage. Despite the fact that my efforts are demanded and expected but not necessarily welcomed.

When my father died I was devastated. My friends and family couldn't understand why I continued to love him, given he'd abandoned us. I suspect when my mother passes I'll mostly experience a heightened sense of relief. That strikes me as very sad, but it's a solid indication of the ongoing burden she has been. I've spent almost 40 years 'carrying' this woman who bore me.

Recommended Tactics

I appreciate my mother's finer qualities now (as I didn't when I was younger), but internally have little patience for her behaviors. She has called me *"stupid"* and an *"idiot"* during our drives to church. My friend who witnesses her cantankerous unruliness affirms I have the patience of a saint. They say patience is a virtue. As a coping mechanism, it's certainly second to none in my opinion.

I've made numerous efforts to understand my mother's perspective. Essentially I disagree with the majority of her choices. I love her, but don't respect her. I honor her dutifully, and won't relinquish my responsibilities to her or my siblings. However, I now require that they share the load. NO, Mum, I will NOT move in or share a home with you. But I will help you start to think about a long term care facility, for example. I will assist (practically and financially) with your funeral and interment decisions to alleviate your concerns about being a burden in death.

There's no question in my mind you'll be missed. The dogs and cats like to be fussed over. Your great-grandchildren (all 5) enjoy playing Dominoes, or chatting with you. Your eldest grandson enjoys family games. Your youngest grandson isn't so much into games, but still appreciates that you support him in cadets, sports and school. Your eldest granddaughters enjoy your company. Your youngest granddaughters don't know you as well, but would share in their father's grief (your eldest son who will be somewhat lost without you). Your youngest son will wear his sorrow like a badge of honor and may have trouble replacing you in his life. You're one of my sister's best friends and she loves you dearly — even if you drive her to distraction with worry or frustration.

Lessons Learned

We might as well resign ourselves to it… You're here to stay until you decide otherwise, or God does. And I believe that God never sends us more than we can bear. We'll cope — you and I — and co-exist as best we can for today and tomorrow, as yesterday. One day at a time. Waiting… patiently and with good humor…

Waiting in the "waiting place" as Dr. Seuss calls it in *Oh The Places You Will Go* — waiting for a train to go, or a bus to come, or a plane to go, or the mail to come, or the rain to go, or the phone to ring, or the snow to snow, or waiting around for a "yes" or "no" or waiting for their hair to grow. Everyone (there) is just waiting. Waiting for the fish to bite, or waiting for wind to fly a kite, or waiting around for Friday night, or waiting, perhaps, for their Uncle Jake, or a pot to boil, or a "better break", or a string of pearls, or a pair of pants, or a wig with curls, or "another chance." Everyone (here) is just waiting.

I hope and pray that **my** children read and remember the rest of the story. I don't want them or me to get "stuck" in the "Waiting Place".

In the meantime, I rarely feel guilty anymore these days. In itself, this is an achievement. My mother excels at passing guilt our way. Like a child might, she tries to maneuver us to get what she wants – even if it means sub-consciously pitting sibling against sibling.

There are boundaries I need to re-establish either before or through her death. I'm developing better ones as I simplify our relationship with honesty. I increasingly refuse to be manipulated through drama into major decisions.

My Story: The Petulant, or What Do You Do When the Terrible Two's Continue into the Awful Eighties

With my mother's health in severe decline, I made probably one of **the** largest decisions of my 54 years so far. Namely, to whole-sale re-enter my parents' excruciating household. This was in order to hold vigil plus to ease for both the build-up to her last day on April 17th, 2010.

> *"I am convinced that, except in a few extraordinary cases, one form or another of an unhappy childhood is essential to the formation of exceptional gifts."* (Thornton Wilder)

Even those who know me well will never fully comprehend the **toll** that one resolution **alone** wreaked upon me. Words are truly inadequate to convey the overwhelming nausea that welled up in the face of putting so **much** of my life on hold for a period exceeding two years.

Let me see if I can possibly describe what that deliberate choice meant and means:

- Setting aside all lingering past hurt to "be with" my mother (over whom I struggled inwardly for decades due to the extreme agony I grew up with at her hands). The image is best depicted as standing next to her withered form with the compassion of a Mother Teresa rather than my former Joan of Arc warrior woman with lance out-thrust on a charging white steed. The armour has been divested and the sword laid to rest.

• Returning to the arena of my most profoundly wounding childhood experiences. Even today as I cross the threshold of that vintage-1963 home, I can easily summon the recessed memories embedded within the very fabric and paint of the rooms. It literally sickens me.

• Accompanying my father and mother on distressing hospital visits to salve an almost-untreatable litany of mounting ailments. The behaviour of both parents on those appointments is unspeakable. You wouldn't believe it. Let's put the horrific scenario like this: If the attending medical professionals hadn't a credo impelling their performance, I'm certain they would've walked away in disgust. Evidence my private dialogues with her doctor and nurses. I don't blame them.

• Listening to my father's bottom-less recitations of puffed-up former grandeur. The man has become an energy cannibal who sucks others' reserves like bones. Trust me. I exaggerate not.

Are you stunned? Disbelieving, you're puzzled, *"Is that how you really feel about your folks, Carol-Ann?"* Yes.

I know I'm blunt. As expressed with a treasured colleague recently, on a self-declaration scale of 1 (low) to 100 (high), my score resides at approximately 200.

Understand why I travel to such lengths to peel back the deepest and potentially-darkest places in my interior. To free you likewise! As Marianne Williamson so eloquently writes in *A Return to Love*, when we let our own light shine we give others permission at the same time. In this instance, it's the contrary but same phenomenon... In so vividly showing you my warts, I hope you'll gain the gumption to be human, too.

Having revealed this much let me go farther. There's more??? For sure!

It should come as no surprise that when I received "The Call" from my father that began with *"I regret to inform you, Carol-Ann…"* I knew how to complete his sentence. I shed no tears. I'd been anticipating it for years.

Really, how could a person not weep over the passing of the woman who gave her life? *"You must be the most heartless of creatures, Carol-Ann."* Not so! It's simply that all floodgates out my eyes had long ago withered into a desert. I was At Peace. If anything, my only soulful torment occurred on Mother's Day of all days… May 9th was my paternal grandmother's birthday but not a good one to arrive at the dawning of a new 'light bulb'… Namely, I never fully had a mother in the first place. Oh, my…

Yes, I had the woman who gave birth to me. Yes, I had the woman who followed to the letter the culture's prevalent scripts about how to raise a child born in 1958. In no fashion, however, did I have a Mom who was responsive to the infant, child, teenager or young woman I actually was. She never did grasp Who I Really Am.

Thank goodness this devastating insight didn't prevent me from addressing those gathered at her service on April 24th. Without reserve, I requested to eulogize my mother. A pitifully small group assembled in the sunlit cemetery chapel. How sad. Having transitioned at age 89, it was a merciful release from a tortured battle with escalating suffering until she finally surrendered her iron clutch upon a largely tragic lifetime. Picture veined skin and boney claw-like fingers clinging desperately to this plane.

Given how I felt about her in my heart-of-hearts (in spite of having taken an intensive forgiveness course just weeks before her passing), you might wonder how did I reconcile the words that crossed my lips with my inner veracity.

Here's how. I coined the term "gracious integrity" to denote the qualities I sought to embody. GRACIOUS in this phrase suggests kindness and a distinct generosity of spirit. INTEGRITY has to do with truthfulness and a certain sense of honor.

Combined, I was able to draw out real examples of her efforts to be my mother while stopping short of feigning genuine love. You can be astonished if you like that I could not bring myself to utter the words (then): *"I love you, Mommy."*

I offer this unflattering peek beneath my kimono to give any of you with ambivalent feelings toward one or both parents complete latitude to admit this reality to yourself (you're in my circles and I know I'm not alone in the broader world on this one). It's OK. No bolt of lightning from the angry gods will hunt you down and strike you dead!

If the facts be told, my father and I each found my eulogy therapeutic for different reasons. He felt my speech paid homage to my mother's memory visibly and in public; being a 'good' daughter reflected well upon him. I'm pleased I had the perspicacity to take advantage of a one-shot deal; the moment would not return and I didn't want to live in regret.

Such a complex chapter of life 2010 and 2011 have been... Let me shed some further light.

During my mother's final miserable months, I also intriguingly reconfirmed the inextricable link between mind-body-spirit. Even I have to remark, *"Oh, my goodness!"* If it was not me encountering what I'm about to portray, I would be even more curious. As it is, it's both challenging and curative to notice how feelings can so directly show up in the physical body.

Never before in my life – and I'm positive never again – will I manifest such clearly painful assaults associated with a particular organ.

For Louise Hay fans out there, we're talking the gall bladder. In her seminal book, *You Can Heal Your Life*, its emotional associations are condemnation and pride. According to my intuition, these attacks were caused by blocked bile. Un-released rage... Gall...

Starting on January 30, 2010 (about a week before my decision to go full-tilt into the parental disaster zone), I had what I call my first Stomach Knot. Within seconds of biting into a delicious pizza slice, it felt like an indigestible dough-ball had landed with a thud at the pit of my abdomen. This resulted in one of those bathroom bouts we all detest; every orifice disgorged into the toilet. I thought it to be the food.

I now know it was not. As it turns out, January 30th fell one week before my father's frantic February 7th call – at his wit's end in the decade-long care of my frail mother. My presaging antennae were already picking up what was to come. That call validated what I needed to do – step back into the shambles I prayed I'd escaped through marriage.

Across February, I manifested further knots – much to my chagrin. Often intolerant of others' hypochondria-based aches and pains, if you could lift the lid off my impatient thoughts, I'd be spouting, *"Get over it!"*

Even during a short fun-filled Las Vegas respite in early March (generously gifted to me and his friends by my cousin to offer temporary relief from the arduous responsibilities) my stomach clenched again. The episode didn't destroy the trip, but it was most disturbing.

Commensurate 100% with parental visits across the spring, I would alternately tighten up and release…

The knots finally arose with such regularity that I made a doctor's appointment on May 31st. Those who know me well realize how much I hate going. So, you can appreciate how seriously I must've been viewing all those incidences. Indeed, that last Monday in May 2010 represented one of the worst vice-grips yet. A blood test revealed no virus. Once an ultrasound confirmed sludge on June 15th I determined the Stomach Knot had gone far enough!

In the five minutes it took me to walk from doctor's office to home, I declared it would be so! Then and there!

You see, as a Reiki Master (a healing modality to clear blockages within and around the body's energy centers) I knew that if my emotions had progressed to such an extent as to show up in the physical body, this was very dangerous. Disease first appears in the etheric body surrounding our visible form. By the time illness takes hold in the physical realm, things are advanced.

Indomitably, I would wrest back my compromised health stemming from damaging emotions regarding my mother's and father's support. At age 52, I deemed I couldn't afford to let matters deteriorate.

Yes, *"I'm free of The Knot"* constituted my strong pronouncement to the Universe! So, you can imagine what a terrible blow it was to return to a violent unexpected episode on August 14th – two months since my firm commitment to never again experience this awful ailment. And once more on August 21st!!

"What the Hell is going on", I asked myself. I answered.

Mid–August was about literally not being able to take in nurturing a great friend offered. She'd gone to great lengths to concoct an incredible menu of extravagant courses. Awfully, I couldn't keep down the food. There's an associated issue with receiving kindness here, but that's a whole other topic! Maybe another book!

In hindsight, August 2010 was littered with several resentful paternal visits. Unquestionably, we'd shared a series of calm cleaning times across the early summer – and made measurable progress in regaining some semblance of order inside and outdoors. However, I'd also pushed the envelope – hugely – when I offered to go to my mother's graveside August 1st on what would have been her 90th birthday. That was the root cause.

Through continued analysis of the Stomach Knot, I've come to identify several core triggers: food; stressors in my overall life; eldercare; and emotions. Of late, it has come to my attention big-time that whether I fail to embrace either positive (joy, passion, exuberance) or so-called negative feelings (anger, frustration, disappointment), I can manifest the symptoms. Mind-blowing!

Contrary to the unhelpful agreement certain acquaintances share with my doctor (that the sludge will inevitably lead to gall stones and surgery), I vehemently disagree! I possess the power to conquer this thing, and wrestle it to the ground I shall!

No one will convince me this knotty "emotional guidance system" isn't merely a temporary trend – strictly endemic to this exceptional phase. I'm certain it will also pass – permanently – once my father has transitioned and I have moved on. Wait and see!

I reiterate: Why do I divulge such intimate detail concerning my 'adventures' with both Un-cope-able Parents? Correct! So you'll feel comfortable according yourself full liberty to experience whatever feelings want to come up when you entertain supporting your loved ones. Wide berth!

The Hidden Opportunity

I think you can see from all I've shared so far that devolution in my father's state has absolutely occurred year over year. In fact, decay is now measured month over month – if not even shorter increments.

> *"I realized it was love, not sadness, that I had bottled up in childhood and that I now needed to give plus express."*
> (Rick Hanson)

In 2010, my Dad was "Mr. Man-About-Town" – quite vital, picking up supplies at the garden center, driving to the bank, buying his groceries at the hot-food counter solo. *"I might be a carpenter and window-washer, but I'm not a cook"* was flirtingly whispered in a conspiratorial tone with women serving his chicken, sausages, carrots and potatoes. What a riot!

Skip ahead to 2011 and you'll find us together at the BBQ counter. Proud Papa loving to put me on display for all to see… After all, he must be this great father if his daughter supports him so… I guess every story has two sides. We'll have gone grocery shopping via taxi – his now-standard mode of transportation. I'll have carefully unpacked his purchases in the upstairs refrigerator. While we take a breather from the outing, I'll be cooking him precisely 18 hard-boiled eggs.

(A side note to mothers everywhere: It's a good thing my paternal grandmother is no longer alive. For, I would be giving her a stern lecture right about now as to the debilitating legacy she created by molly-coddling my father until he married at age 36 – resulting in the ridiculous truth that he doesn't even know how to boil an egg for himself! If you have a son, please teach him to cook and clean as you would a daughter! Sorry about the rant – but really…)

Seeing and feeling how exponentially my Dad has come to rely on me since my mother's passing, I can locate genuine compassion within my core.

Ironically, his descent has brought forth a number of special "gifts". Please forgive my being graphic. Otherwise, the exchange will lose a measure of its poignancy.

Appalled at the state of my father's hygiene, I adamantly resisted a last vestige of paternal privacy in 2010 and stayed away from laundering his under-garments. Do NOT ask how he survived; you don't want to know.

Let's just say that in his diminishing state, I've come to realize the wash isn't going to get done any more than driving is going to take place – not unless he accedes to having the local dry cleaners do it for him. That isn't going to happen. Unless I do the dastardly deed, they'll remain in filth. Yuck. Friends who are concerned about my interests stringently warned I should not do it. I understand why.

Funny enough, the first round of shorts through my parents' 1970's washer (if you can imagine!) had me convinced this, too, will be a healing process for us both.

(To all you manufacturers of so-called high-efficiency modern machines, I stubbornly declare: *"Nothing beats the old-fashioned spinner and wash line for cleanliness!"*)

Given my weak stomach, can you possibly conceptualize what it took to handle those grimy pants?? Without a word of a lie, I dug out a large towel from my mother's linen closet and wrapped it around my nose and mouth, so that only my eyes were showing. A laundry bandit! With thick medical gloves left behind by her nurse – I dove in – spraying pre-wash like a crazed woman. You have my permission to smile at the image.

During the main cycle, I wandered into the recreation room-bunker where he holes up to ponder: *"How did Mommy ever stand to hand-wash my diapers?"* Without skipping a beat, my father stated: *"Well, that's just the nature of a mother's love for her baby. When she sees her infant grow week by week, nothing else counts. She can set aside the rest, because she gains so much satisfaction from raising a healthy baby."*

Holy smokes!! I was stunned. I'd never looked at it this way. The man made sense! I returned to the laundry room with a huge grin beneath my towel-mask. For all his foibles that drive me bats, we'd just shared a magical moment. I shall never forget it.

Such is the hidden opportunity of this transitional phase.

Despite myself, I must confess to looking forward on a certain level to our few remaining precious conversations before he goes. "The Laundry Chat" demonstrates incisive lucidity. Particularly since my mother never understood me, it's like my father is offering a priceless treasure on both their behalves during his waning years.

While we clearly live on borrowed time, I further recognize he's attempting to imprint final words of wisdom. Perhaps he's scared I'll forget the many lessons with which he has blessed me across the decades. I won't.

When we part ways now, he makes sure to express all the love he feels for me in his heart and soul; I reply in kind. He regularly references *"how thrilled Mommy was coming out of the doctor's office when she learned she was expecting you, Carol-Ann"*. I accept his points.

While needing none of his paternal protectiveness, he's always concerned that I'll be safe riding transit home alone; this, during daytime hours.

Yes, you never know when a miracle is going to fly at you from left field.

Contrary to the graveside visit of August 2010, I was positively surprised to muster a lump in my throat while standing before my mother's marker in 2011. I stuffed down my tears to not upset my father, but it was reassuring to know I possess the ability to summon loving maternal feelings after all. I rather liked the warm and fuzzy feeling of reaching into my gentle core.

You see, to survive constant emotional assault, I had plated my tender interior behind invisible metallic shields. This served to protect as much as possible against further damage, but it also sealed my heart behind iron-strong casing; good things were barricaded from reaching me.

That's why it surprises yet pleases me that I now frequently see, hear and feel my mother trying to support me from The Other Side.

My Grandma is also with me in my office. Just as my mother's family was hovering above her bed waiting to welcome her back to Heaven… Any of you who believe in the watchfulness of departed relatives and friends will readily accept what I'm sharing. You don't have to. What I'm sure about is that my mother accompanies me strongly every time my favorite radio station plays Janet Jackson's song, *Together Again*. It's her way of reminding me that family members are trying to help my father cross over.

You never know. That's why it's so vital to stay open to possibility.

Net-net, I plan to continue in the fashion my father and I have evolved our relationship – for what I hope will be his remaining short future. I stand in trust that all is well on a higher plane.

A precious friend expressed it well: *"I think you have chosen to walk with your father as he gets ready to transition partially out of obligation but also because it is the path you have chosen. Sometimes walking with someone is neither easy nor fulfilling for one party. But the lessons we learn about ourselves in retrospect will be worthwhile."* Correct!

Patrick's words bring to mind a fascinating team-building facilitation conducted in September 2010 at a sumptuous mature lifestyles residence. From the gorgeous décor to the nourishing meals to the afternoon socializing to the interactions with staff I could bear witness to – I said to myself: *"Bring it on! Every need seems to be met in this place – right down to the hair salon and barber shop. You mean you can get a weekly manicure – something that doesn't even happen at my age?"*

In the same breath, however, I remember the stooped ladies and gentlemen plotting their rickety courses across the public areas hunched over their walkers. Safety precautions may have necessitated it. Still, the image struck me as rather pathetic and in stark contrast to the luxurious surroundings.

Deep down, I'm convinced my father is somehow connected to his personal soul contract. Perhaps there's an odd wisdom after all in remaining in his home – ludicrous as that may sound after all the tales I've recounted.

My Plea

Will you indulge me in a heartfelt supplication?

Please, please, please…Baby Boomers…let us not become like the WWII Generation when we age. Our golden years do not need to – and **should not** – become like those of our folks. Read: narrow-minded, shrunken and fearful.

> *"Life is not meant to be a journey to the grave with the intention of arriving safely, attractively coiffed, perfectly manicured, body weak and stymied, wings down and tail dragging under but rather to skid in sideways, hair flying in your wave, wings fully un-furled, chest up, eyes sparkling, chocolate in one hand, wine in the other, body thoroughly enjoyed, totally worn out and screaming – Woo Hoo! What a ride!"* (Anonymous)

Instead, I'm earnestly begging ALL my contemporaries – especially those who are themselves parents – we **must** strive to be FAR more gracious and dignified once we reach the stage of life our parents occupy.

Think ancient practices wherein elders – bearing a regal maturity befitting their station – were revered community leaders toward whom younger generations willingly deferred.

You know, on more than one occasion, interviewees noted how selfish can be The Greatest Generation. I concur. In so very many ways, they do make it "all about them". Disconcerting given the tremendous sacrifices they voluntarily endured to create a world they prayed would be free of tyranny for their own children…

Perhaps they've come to believe it's now their God-given right to demand something back from us. Well, I'm here to say there's a very great difference between ordering and asking. Yes, conscience would dictate what's right by those who gave us life. However, this doesn't necessarily translate into automatic entitlement in the form of self-centeredness.

As a distinguished aging neighbor living a few houses north of my father remarked in March 2012 (knowing I've been sustaining overnighters and consistent parental visits for over two years): *"It's patently unfair that your father uses* (to be interpreted as takes extreme advantage) *you like this. You have a long commute to get here and his opposing personality is very trying. Does he realize what a huge burden all this puts upon you?"* No.

Even if they're oblivious, we (their children) are **very** aware of the toll our obdurate parents' support extracts. Do you want to put your progeny through anything close to the turmoil you survive in the face of your parents' stuck attitudes??

Truly, their unspoken and unrealistic expectations place an unfair burden on the Sandwich Generation as we run around ragged by the care of young and old alike.

Thus, when loved ones one day see our vitality waning and gently bring up the subject of transition into the next *"chapter of life"*, let's adopt a spirit of collaboration. How about we listen with open ears rather than the suspicious minds that typically greet our outreaches to the current elderly?

For your offspring's sakes and ours, I offer my plea.

In case you're thinking I'm doling out sour grapes – not at all. Don't take only my word. Listen in as a dear friend heart-wrenchingly describes her conflicted struggles in striving to be charitable toward her headstrong mother:

"We're overwhelmed between our kids, our parent(s) and our grandchildren.

Neediness is excused in the very young. Dealing with it, raising children, seems to come naturally. I guess dependence should be excused in the very old, too. That will include us soon enough. However, we never learned about caring for seniors – especially not while balancing our family lives.

It's a very different kind of need, a very demanding one that grows so as you get older, not less. We have a responsibility to pass these new skills on to our children in this age of elders. Elder abuse abounds today. The social problem has become a personal one.

Mother, like a child, you seek attention, positive or negative. Like a child, you act out on impulse particularly if you don't get what you want. You have called me names such as 'fractious child'. Like a child, you seek to secure your independence but aren't responsible for your actions. You've become a bit of a bully.

When we indulge you, it's with the knowledge that we are only buying ourselves a moment's peace, maybe. We can teach you nothing as you are not interested in learning from us, only from Oprah. Our patience and concern are not investments in our future as they are with our children and theirs. We don't know if you realize that, not having had the opportunity to care for your own aging parents.

Then again, if we think of our efforts as wasted time, how will that change when we are the aged and the ones needing support? Will we expect our children to pay us back in kind? Will we be conscious of the effects on their lives? Will we recognize when we become a burden? Will we be ready to let go? Will we, like you, live vicariously through our children, or theirs?

Or will we find new and exciting things to live for, to learn? Make new friends? Laugh a lot? Even share a love with a partner, new or old? Will we volunteer to help those less fortunate than us? Will we develop strong friendships with all members of our family equally, regardless of age or gender, and sometimes against the odds? Will we seek first to understand? Will we do those things that we have encouraged you to do, and think we have failed to achieve?

After all, there's a life lesson to be learned here. It might be different if we didn't have children of our own. We do. And they're growing up.

Yet even if we didn't have offspring, we would still have a social responsibility, wouldn't we? We are all part of the world's transition to a larger population, an aged population. Some people like you, Mum, soon to leave this world, aren't adapting well. Some don't want that responsibility.

I wonder how much that will have changed in 30 years, when I reach the age you are now?"

Thanks, Mishka. You've helped me bring forth these important points before I burst! Couldn't have said it better myself.

In case you need a more light-hearted take on these same themes, here it is in the form of an email joke sent me called "Senior Moments". Enjoy!

"Hospital regulations require a wheel chair for patients being discharged. However, while working as a student nurse, I found one elderly gentleman already dressed and sitting on the bed with a suitcase at his feet who insisted he didn't need my help to leave the hospital. After a chat about rules being rules, he reluctantly let me wheel him to the elevator. On the way down, I asked if his wife was meeting him. 'I don't know', he said. 'She's still upstairs in the bathroom changing out of her hospital gown'."

The Saga Continues

This chapter of my journey is by no means done. Since the summer of 2010, here are just

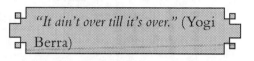

"It ain't over till it's over." (Yogi Berra)

a few of the numerous alarming hits and highlights of "Life with Father":

- A shocking incident while backing out of his driveway in which both feet were unequivocally positioned on the accelerator (based on careful reconstruction I undertook in my mind afterwards). This resulted in a rocket-fast careen straight out and in reverse up the street until control prevailed and he shut down the motor at the base of the neighbor's drive. To this day, my father will vociferously deny that the error was human. He'll insist the gas pedal stuck. I was there to know differently. Even though a non-driver, I'm well-enough informed to realize the truth. Trust me, it was his mistake.

- You're already aware of the failed first 'driving' test in November 2010. Together, these scenarios had a significant destructive effect upon his story of being a stellar driver from before age 16 to 88.

- Fast-forward to March 2011. Away on business travels at the time, all I know through what Derek was able to extricate and I was able to subsequently glean, there was at minimum one mishap in a local parking lot involving his 1995 Buick Roadmaster — a tank-like vehicle under the best of conditions. Police and a tow-truck sound like they were dispatched. Does that give you a sense? Apparently, my Dad was turning into a parking space (and I suspect stepping on the gas yet again), resulting in a 'bump' to the adjoining car plus the one next to it. Oh, my God…There remains a nebulous mystery concerning smashed-in headlights on his 1987 Cutlass during this same period…

- Next, let me take you to February 2012 – and the loaded subject of expiring auto insurance on my father's two vehicles. Apart from potentially incurring $4,000 in fees (which a senior, even on a teacher's solid pension, would be wise to avoid), why even "go there"??? To entertain renewal would have been a strictly ego-based move. Very costly just to boost his already bombastic arrogance! Given all these harrowing incidents, is anyone thinking, why debate the subject at all???

Or, perhaps you're screaming in your head: *"Take away his d--n car keys!"* I hear you!!

Here's the deal.

If we go back to the **LOVING ACTION** of **Trust**, I believe with all my might that everything is unfolding in its own course.

No, I'm not being an ostrich with its proverbial head in the sand. Just as my Dad knows me for 53 years, I know him for 30-plus as an adult.

On the heels of the March 2011 repairs, my father has not gotten behind the wheel since. He claims he's just waiting *"until things settle down a bit."* Then, he'll experiment by spinning each vehicle around the block *"to make sure it's in working order."* Believe me when I say we both know he'll never drive again. He needs to repeat these weary phrases to save face. He has no intention to trot out either car. Thank the Lord!

Nonetheless, being a fully Un-cope-able Parent, we initially had to go through a whole harangue to unwind his ill-fated intentions. There's no easy surrender when it comes to my father. Are you kidding? No way! Like every one of my other hard-won "conquests", I had to plot out an elaborate scheme to shut down this latest ordeal – particularly in light of his over-inflated opinions of driving prowess.

Want to know what I did? I called his insurance carrier behind his back to obtain facts and details. So often, I can sense I've worn out my welcome with the agency head due to my myriad questions designed to forestall any possible objection which my father could mount.

For a merciful nanosecond, I thought we stopped him in his tracks. I should be so lucky! Once we discovered he's considered an active driver with the Ministry of Transportation until October 2012 (because of unjustifiably squeaking past the authorities in 2010), it was back to the drawing board.

What my father doesn't bargain on yet anyone who knows me can confirm – I'm most definitely his daughter in the strong-willed department. He has met his match.

Though, I must concede ingenious credit to the man for the number of countervailing strategies he was able to summon when we sat down to talk! He threw in red herrings having more to do with home than vehicular insurance. He suggested maybe he should start up both cars *"just to test the batteries"*. Nope! *"I don't think that's a good idea, Daddy."* He looked crestfallen. So be it. He's a hazard!

These old folks sure can be clever when they want to! He stumped me a few times, but I tried not to let on. As soon as I got home, I asked Derek what the "right answer" was! Roaring!

Somehow, the Angels were on my side and we managed to skate past that crisis. My father's attention is now diverted by new matters like getting the garden *"back in shape"* – which he will not have the energy to do. Another fable he needs to tell himself to feel OK.

Finally, should he utter a peep anymore about this topic, I will be on him like a duck on a June bug!

If you can imagine, I'm reciting only the major episodes! Too countless to tally, I should yet note the growing instances of multiple calls per day that start at hours like 5:30 a.m. because he just *"has to"* say what's on his mind in *that* moment. He can't wait to speak until our daily afternoon phone schedule. Totally like an impatient tot barking from the car's back seat every few seconds: *"Are we there yet?"* Or, the times he's forgotten our planned visits and then gotten mad at me for *"catching"* him with his pajamas still on at 3:00 in the afternoon! Last time I looked, I'm not standing there for my health.

Given the continued endurance **test** my father's support proves to be, I'm not one bit ashamed that I've learned to regularly reach out to my network of friends when it all gets too much. I gain much-needed soothing and nurturing. Often, it's simply to vent for a few minutes.

Some people may see my strategy as a sign of weakness – like I can't handle it on my own. I choose to view this relatively new coping mechanism on my part as a distinct mark of strength. I've always "gone it alone" in my life. I struggled in stoic silence through my father's former alcoholism and my mother's mental illness. Martyrdom is no longer for me!

Interestingly, ongoing emotional support in the form of safe friends or others is the same counsel renowned coach, Cheryl Richardson offered in one of her weekly online newsletters – this time, dealing with the topic of Aging Parents. (Check her out, as she always has something of value to share.)

Cheryl urges us to experience **all** our feelings – even the so-called inappropriate ones (such as wishing your folks would pass so the insanity will stop). I love it! I've been there! Guilty as some might want to make me for even having the thought!

Then again, those folks aren't the right ones to entrust with the overwhelming roller-coaster ride eldercare can be. Definitely not! You need someone who listens well and does **NOT** offer unsolicited opinions.

No matter your relationship – good or poor – with your parents, you will need to grieve the loss of who they once were.

Therefore, my wish in offering these snippets from just a few of the MANY meaningful emails pasted into an over-flowing journal is that they will provide you with soothing similar to that which I experienced when they arrived.

"Carol-Ann, you are very brave. You are being honest with yourself, with your father and with others. Many people are incapable of your level of integrity. I think you know that in your heart of hearts. Carol-Ann has courage, though, to face her inner self, and deal with her feelings, knowing them for what they are. You are a conscious observer of life, at its best and worst. That doesn't mean you must become a cynic, however. Keep looking for the rainbows – they follow a storm. Breathe. Just breathe."

"You are being your authentic self – living your story before you finish writing it. It takes guts to do what you're doing with your life right now. Warrior woman indeed! Fighting life's battles and winning (not just surviving). There is something Amazonian about you. Maintaining your spirit. Your love of life. Despite what many people would hide under a gloss of 'making the best of things' or 'dutiful filial sorrow', you soldier on, bearing your true feelings with refreshing candor and grace. You are handling this transition with great aplomb, as you should, as you must."

"You are going through a very difficult period in your life where the parent becomes the stubborn child who doesn't want to listen…I know it isn't funny for the person going through it, but some day you will look back and see humor in the little things that are happening right now. Other things will bring you back to the fast boiling point – for quite a while after even these things fade in their intensity. You will also find your mind holding onto the smiles and little nuances that you will share on this final journey."

In addition to these touching messages, I admit to relishing these friends' remarks. They remind me entirely of my reality:

"…never a dull moment when we step through the threshold of life with the door marked…'Yes, I will be Present in my Own Life'… I never saw the door marked 'Drag your heels and no one will notice'. Alas, in the end it was always my choice what door to turn 'ye olde' handle and check it out… My preference is to flame out at the top of my senior game as it were, rather than have an account at the local drug mart hoping I can get a deal on a power-assist chair… I don't need any reminding that existing and living are

two very different approaches to your senior years. To my friend's mother, I would say right on, yeah keep up that legacy of living till you're 90 with the primary goal of making everyone around you miserable…!"

"Old women like my mother (she's only 79, but she's been practicing to be a crotchety old lady since her forties!) resist taking advantage of help, even if it is available and they really need it, sometimes because they simply believe that only a family member can and should provide the services."

See what I mean about what AMAZING buddies I have?

Fascinatingly, these endorsing and moving emails consistently land in my inbox when I feel most like I could scream. How synchronistic! If not sometimes for others' championship, I wonder where I'll find the strength to see things through to the finish line.

Yet, all the while my father languishes, it's fascinating to observe how new lessons and updated strategies arrive in the nick of time. For example, just as I was about to undertake the excruciating visit called "The Car Conversation" (where I was prepared to stop at nothing to prevent my father from EVER driving again) a crystal-clear equation came to me:

Compassion + Clarity = Results

Based on what I've already said about **Intention** within LOVING and **Initiate** under ACTION, this formula seems simply another expression. Nonetheless, it served me in February 2012 to learn to take the good with the bad. A dear friend says it better than I: *"This is just another lesson in loving, caring and letting go for both your Father and yourself."* I agree.

My strong intuition is that my Dad and I are being given a short amount of bought-time to guarantee no syllable is left un-uttered by the date of his imminent passing.

Toward that end – though deeply frustrated in April – I managed to find the wherewithal to offer a sincere declaration. Namely, I thanked him for making Easter a special childhood occasion by sprinkling garden dirt inside the recreation room threshold in recognition of my awe over the bunny's baskets-full of chocolate treats! This – during an era when money was tight... How cute. How poignant.

Friends feel it was kind of me to acknowledge my father's generosity. I believe it was important for him to know that despite all his foibles (and mine!) I remember and appreciate from the bottom of my heart and soul everything he has meant to me.

I remain certain this will allow my Daddy to cross the threshold to The Other Side with a measure of serenity and knowing that he always did his best.

We'll see where this last lap leads us. Only time will tell what fate has left in store.

Addendum

Yes indeed, we never quite know what destiny reserves for any of us. I find this a mixed blessing.

For, if we human beings could presage every event around the next corner, we might easily reject the advent of certain developments well before they came close to arrival. Such is the case with a sudden and unexpected sequence of crises on July 23, 2012 – well into this book's production processes.

On that afternoon, my father was hospitalized – rescued at my hands from his questionable "living" conditions and entering Emergency on death's doorstep. Oh, my goodness.

Since, his seemingly-interminable lingering through this latest form of suffering is almost more intolerable than his oft-ridiculous insistence to expire in his hovel. Rather than being carted out in the back of a hearse (his desire as far back as I can remember), he was hauled out on an ambulance stretcher in the nick of time.

I must confess to actively praying for his quick demise – as does his attending physician since that ill-fated afternoon. We share a speechless astonishment over the will to exist despite all counter-indications.

Just as this volume is not intended to be a diatribe about woefully-equipped systems to contend with burgeoning eldercare demands, so too is not a commentary on such moral and ethical issues as euthanasia or otherwise. Each family's decision-making in these regards is so very personal I cannot possibly touch on these finer points.

All I know for sure is, this option would be considered his worst possible, had my father the consciousness to be fully aware of his circumstances. It is entirely devastating to stand at the foot of his bed, as he portrays death warmed over. Though episodes associated with alcoholism and other dysfunctions have been no picnic across 54 years, I declare this last leg takes the cake.

And, I maintain the firm plus clear conviction that anything that now occurs until his final passage will simply reinforce my earnest and capable desire to support all of you battling Un-cope-able Parents. The next time we "see" one another, I look forward to delving into your eyes – mirrors to the soul – and saying: "I hear you. I get it. I empathize. I truly know everything you are thinking, feeling and going through."

My Parting Encouragements to You

Upon reflection, if there were only one statement I could render, it is this:

Try not to take your parents' 'bad' behavior personally.

It's not about you. It's about the tough situation. How easy to say but virtually impossible to do when you have Un-cope-able Parents!

Just remember: If they're difficult, negative, or irritable, it's probably because they're afraid. After all, they're going through their own challenging changes – not the least of which is loss of independence.

Many regress into protective behaviors when under duress. Some go into denial and lose themselves in mindless activities. Others get impatient and wind up brusque. Make that belligerent in my case! Some complain non-stop about every little thing. Not to mention endlessly repeating their past accomplishments.

My father engages in all of these and more!

Through my paternal trials and tribulations, I've additionally come to notice that qualities which characterize us earlier in life become magnified in later years. For example, I've long tended to check my passport and currency a neurotic number of times before embarking on trips – in the same way my father today quadruple-checks his keys and money before setting out on grocery shops.

(Yes, I've already asked my friends to point out my annoying behaviors by pulling me behind the barn and shooting me if I come dangerously close to my parents' paranoia and other outrageously-unattractive attitudes and actions once old!)

Bottom-line, I'm attempting – desperately – to see you not become as far-gone as I was by my exasperating parents until you get a grip. May you experience nothing like my pain-staking lessons in the care of your loved ones!

Yes, every single one of the LOVING ACTION Keys to Coping with Un-cope-able Parents has been excruciatingly achieved. Please remember to take them wherever you go – literally and figuratively.

LOVING

Laughter = Humor truly is the best medicine for ensuring your aging folks don't make you go off-the-wall

Openness = Stay open to the possibility that there exist many potential perspectives on your parents

Vibration = Strive to hold your loved ones as "whole, resourceful and creative" in their Essence, so as to keep your own energy field light

Intention = Examine your interior with diligence to test the purity of your intentions; remember to focus on The Wanted

Neutrality = Maintain a detached stance so as to have zero should-based opinions for your parents; learn to love without attached caring

Grace = Demonstrate grace under pressure so as to be present to your folks' needs and not miss opportunities to lower their aged stress levels

ACTION

Advocate = Create a safe environment where both parents can speak their truth with you as their mediator

Clarify = Ask plenty of open-ended questions to by-pass parental ploys to withhold critical information

Trust = Find the faith and equanimity to trust all is unfolding in your lives according to a Higher Plan

Initiate = Like it or not, you'll likely to have to intervene in your folks' situation at some point; don't wait for an express invitation

Observe = Listen, watch body language and non-verbal mannerisms to either confirm or disprove your intuitive sense

iNnovate = Constantly seek out-of-the-box solutions to stay one step ahead of your crafty elders

Further Opportunities

COPING Blog

How delicious would it be to exchange with like-minded compatriots those "naughty" thoughts you secretly harbor toward your Un-cope-able Parents? Especially

> "You can trust God not to let you be tried beyond your strength, and with any trial He will give you a way out of it and the strength to bear it." (1 Corinthians 10:13)

so-called "inappropriate" ones like wishing they would pass away! Did you say that out loud? Carol-Ann heard you and totally appreciates your honesty. She doesn't believe for one nanosecond you're "evil" – much as certain critical people would seek to make you. What self-righteous nonsense! Unless someone has walked in your shoes for more than a minute, they have zero permission to command how you "should" feel. At "The Un-cope-ables", you'll have full freedom to express your warts and all. We love them. If your truth is anything like Carol-Ann's, you'll find huge cathartic value from reading others' moving accounts while prevailing over your pig-headed duo. Let's support each other.

COPING Coaching

A Life Coach since 1999, Carol-Ann Hamilton serves as a Crossroads Navigator to clients from their 20's to 60's – igniting them to uncover and live a broader earthly purpose. Specialized in transitions, she knows only too well no other period (save for an infant's understandable demands) will leech such huge energy from your precious stores. If you allow it! Ceaseless aged parents are totally akin to the incessant tot's back seat barking: *"Are we there yet?"* Access her individual and group coaching through Spirit Unlimited at www.CarolAnnHamilton.com. Emerge from this unequivocally draining phase with your physical, emotional and mental stamina intact. Ever your champion and advocate, you will profit from an empathetic sounding board while gently challenging you to release unproductive attitudes so you remain your Best Self throughout the trial and tribulation.

COPING Interviews

You can almost smell the coffee brewing as we wake up to our reality. Eldercare is in a state of crisis. Aging populations are burgeoning – and not just in North America. The urgency is global. Daunting already, wait until the Baby Boomer bulge strains current senior support systems to breakage. Still, nations everywhere remain dismally-equipped to face these alarming implications. That's why the world needs staunch activists to initiate critical public dialogue on these pervasive and invasive issues. Expect the unexpected! Yours won't be a typical interaction with Carol-Ann Hamilton. Your radio and print audiences don't need snore-inducing content and simplistic advice. For those open to receiving out-of-the-box yet grounded tactics from the care-giving "trenches", she delivers incisive ideas that work. Even with parents who are impossible to the power of infinity – like hers!

COPING Speaking Engagements

Carol-Ann is a genuine graduate of the Hard School of Un-cope-able Knocks. Since birth, anguish at her unbearable parents' hands has solidly equipped her to pen this volume. For all the suffering, she thanks them gratefully. How else would she have attained such unique understanding that now promotes comfort in Sandwich Generation contemporaries who endure intolerable aging folks? For your upcoming industry or association event, you can anticipate being alternately inspired and provoked by this seasoned presenter known for her compassionate integrity. Her stories like "The Driving Test" and "The Stolen Garage Door Opener" have to be heard to be believed! It's a collection that expands daily while contending with her cantankerous 89-year-old father. When Carol-Ann is at the helm, you're sure to belly-laugh one moment and stream tears the next.

COPING Workshops

If you'd love the advantage of personalized time while sharing insights in an intimate group setting, then one of Carol-Ann's workshops would be a perfect choice. Of durations ranging from three hours to two days, sessions rest upon the bedrock of her 30 years' expertise in corporate facilitation. With the LOVING ACTION Keys to Coping as her springboard, she happily customizes offerings to suit your special needs. Consistently recognized for her notable gift to create a safe and engaging learning environment, she brings deep listening and caring to the very-contentious subject of how you *really* feel about your elders. As a result of giving voice to your candor, you will significantly transmute your agony; rest assured. A combination of interactive exercises and individual reflection will add tools to your kit while refreshing your spirit to re-enter the parental battlefield.

For more information about Carol-Ann Hamilton and her service offerings, visit www.CarolAnnHamilton.com or call Spirit Unlimited at 905-822-2503.

About the Author

CAROL-ANN HAMILTON is a catalyst, pioneer-visionary and healer who inspires people toward purposefulness in professional and personal life.

Prior to establishing her coaching and facilitation companies – Changing Leadership and Spirit Unlimited – she brought 25 years' experience as an Organizational Development Consultant to a variety of Fortune 500, entrepreneurial and project management settings.

In 2003, she spread her wings and soared beyond cubicle walls to pursue her true calling. At the time, this "cold turkey" decision constituted an enormous leap of faith. It was just one of many bold actions emblematic of Carol-Ann's particular brand of courage that has earned her a loyal following amongst clients, colleagues and friends alike.

Today, organizations from diverse sectors rely on her performance coaching, change management and team building expertise to foster meaningful environments while attaining bottom-line prosperity. Through her consulting efforts across North America, in selected Caribbean and Australian locations, this thought leader promotes leaders to call forth results.

Co-author of *The A to Z Guide to Soul Inspiring Leadership* and by-invitation contributor to *The Courage to Succeed, Walking With The Wise for Entrepreneurs* and *Expert Women Who Speak, Speak Out!* it wasn't until she penned *Step Out of Your Sandbox!* that Carol-Ann felt she fully came into her own.

Over the five years the latter took to compose, she released so many stale comfort zones she doesn't even know where the box is anymore! Since that publication in 2010, she relished in tons of fun creating *The Pissed-Off Journal* – her irreverent tool to help people let go of the annoying events of daily life in three easy steps based on her lifelong struggles with anger management.

Now – heralded by a singular conversation – the arrival of *Coping with Un-cope-able Parents: LOVING ACTION for Eldercare* earmarks her most profound work yet. Carol-Ann fervently hopes this deeply personal yet widely applicable work will form a ground-breaking blueprint to support the Baby Boomer generation sandwiched between their own growing families' imperatives and the bottomless neediness of demanding elderly parents. It is for you that she offers her heartfelt, hard-won keys to success.

It is safe to say, nothing delights this spiritual warrior more than enthusing others to unleash their potential by sharing her experiences – evidenced by her motto *"Encouraging Your Greatness"*. When her earthly sojourn ends at age 112, Carol-Ann's bone-deep wish is that humanity the world over will have reclaimed its inner magnificence.

To learn more about how you can access this Transformation Agent's offerings, go to http://www.CarolAnnHamilton.com. You can also follow Carol-Ann on **Facebook, LinkedIn, Twitter@ GetUnstuckNow, and YouTube.**